Understanding Your Choice

ETTA D. JACKSON

All inquiries should be addressed to: Etta D. Jackson
mail: arcanum33@gmail.com
Phone: +1 917 667-8511
Website: http://www.ancientmysterybooks.com

Book editing: Jacqueline A. Routier-von Felbert
Contributing editors: Cara Quinn and Kathryn Riach
Reproduction of illustrations: Dawn Browning

Masonic Images: Mr. Laziz Hamani

Library of Congress Control Number: 2004108468
International Standard Book No. 0-9746101-2-7

First Edition Published in the United States of America by Lapis Communications

Printed in the United States of America

Dedication

This book is dedicated to my grandson Dylan Tyler von Felbert who was born around the same time as the birth of this book.

May they both be Lights to the world.

Table of Contents

Chapter Seven: 177

Acknowledgements

I am exceedingly grateful to these many people who supported me in so many ways over these last seven years. Special thanks go to:

Britton, Alan, Shirley and Alex who understood more than most what my journey to England was about. Thank you for being such gracious hosts to me. To Elizabeth and Victoria, thank you for teaching me to Line Dance. Your help in putting the finishing touches to this book were invaluable.

Burnet, Beverlyan: I like how you give to this work yet not always completely sure if you have the total understanding but because you are so committed to what you know in your soul is your part in an ancient and divine plan, you serve with all your heart. Thank you for being the indirect link to Dr. Whitworth!

Cohort 11, at the California Institute of Integral Studies for each one's participation in our reunion on the planet, what a meeting! To those in the group who contributed to my journey personally, I thank you with all my heart. You were a source of strength at some of the most crucial moments. I love you greatly, all of you.

Dixon, Sonia: your instinctive understanding of your service to the light is unmatched. This gave you the insight to carry out your part in our journeys together. Thanks for all your help.

Evans, Wally: a dear friend who offered me board at a very challenging time. Thanks for your love and support. I will always think of you as a brother.

Ferguson, Rechel: who in my heart will always be a dear sister and friend. The role you played in my life and work will always be remembered.

Gates, Ebu'an: Thanks to you and Charles for being dear friends.

Henessey, Phil: with whom I discovered the Oblesik and sphinxes along the Thames toward London Bridge. I will always remember you as a dear friend. Thanks for all your support.

Isis and Argon: in your unique way, you served as an important link to the many people and places in England and Scotland I needed to visit.

James, Robin: my travel companion throughout England into Edinburgh.

Karolyi, Stephen: wherever you are Stephen, I hope you will one day come to know how greatly you are loved and know that your contributions have added greatly to the work of liberation of souls on this planet.

Kraemer, Michele: Thanks for being the link to Dr. Whitworth. I look forward to the development of our friendship.

Lawal, Babatunde: your gentle spirit and your inner knowledge of your Masonic obligation to this great work make you a valued server in this Aquarian Age of true brotherhood.

Lissauer, Trevor: You are one of those new souls to the planet who represent our future. You have all come in to be a beacon of light to the world. May your music continue to unfold you to your divine purpose here. Thank you.

Liekkio, Mark and Priscilla: I knew when I met you in Bali that we would meet again but had no idea of how our future meeting would play out. Thank you for housing, assistance with the manuscript, publication of this book and for caring in so many ways. Your commitment to the work of the divine plan is unmatched. Love you lots!

Milner, Debbie: it is been my great privilege to know you. The contributions you will make to the world and in particular your Jewish heritage, are most assured. I look forward to our work together. I look forward to our work together.

Nazon, Marie and Ebun: Who would have known Marie that the urgent call for you to go to Africa to help with the Aids epidemic would bring me back to New York to stay in your flat for three months. It was here that I was given the directive to begin writing the book after being given the title 25 years earlier. You even had a book on your bookshelf on how to write a book and a computer on your desk. Thank you for your friendship and your continued support.

Pearce, Tina: Your support is greatly appreciated. Our trip to Stonehenge that early morning in July cannot be forgotten. Thanks to you and family for your sacrifice and continued support.

Quinn, Michael and Cara: Simply, thank you for everything. Have a most sacred life together.

Redwood, Audrey (Joy): you are dear to my heart. Thanks so much for your support and love when you had no idea what I was about or why you needed to house me and especially in the writing of this book. I am sure it is the Aquarian you are.

Renfree, Phil and Sheila: Thanks Sheila for the unique role you played in my travel through Cornwall and especially to those sacred sites that are off the beaten path. To Phil and the rest of the family, I hold you in my heart always.

Routier-von Felbert, Jacqueline: You have been my single greatest teacher. Thanks for the opportunity to be your mother and for the great expansion of consciousness it has offered me. Your home has always been like an oasis on my travels in Europe.

Rozelle, Jimmy and Wendy: You and your family are in my thoughts often. Thank you for being you in your individual differences.

Sam-Esprit, Emmanuel: Thank you so much for all your computer help. I can't imagine how I could have completed this manuscript without your help.

St. Clair, Rick: Thanks for your support, which is invaluable to the next step forward for this book.

Urhobo, Ben, Gina, Lynda and family: I knew when I met you that my re-orientation to the continent of Africa and to Nigeria would come through you. Thanks for the love, support and the links you have established to the work to be done in our Motherland.

van Daam, Renee: A great soul who this world is privileged to have and whose knowledge of self will come with time to the great benefit of the world.

von Felbert, Dirk: to my son-in-law who I love so dearly partly because of our lifetimes together. One day you will know why I am in your life and you in mine. Thank you to Elfie and Werner for their wonderful hospitality and openness and thank you for being you.

Weintraub, Dara: Simply, thank you! The Light of true power and leadership is yours because you dared to open your heart to love.

Whitecliff, Angelika: Your strong inner knowing is the pillars of fire and cloud to guide you by day and night. Thank you for the vision you hold with me for this book.

Wierman, Dan and Pat: who would have known Pat that after meeting you in Bali and Chang Mai we would come together again with my staying with you for over a year. Thank you Dan and Pat for your gracious support and being such wonderful hosts.

Whitworth, Drs. Eugene and Ruth: thanks for support and encouragement you offered and the vision you held for this book coming into physical form.

My thanks for permission to use materials for this book go to Builders of the Adytum in Los Angeles; The Lucis Trust in New York and London; The Philosophical Research Society in Los Angeles, Mr. Laziz Hamani and Aussouline Publishers for permission to use the Masonic symbols: the Compass and the Square, and the All- Seeing Eye of God, from Symbols of Freemasonry. Thanks also to others not mentioned.

Author's Note

This book has emerged out of the collective need of humanity to have a deeper understanding of his life and experiences here on planet Earth. When this book was given to me to write in 1975, I wrote the title down as I was directed, and looking at these three words: 'Understanding Your Choice', I thought what an odd title for a book. What could anyone write about such a title? I dismissed the whole thing and went on with my life. However, every five to ten years the title would pop up in my memory. Then in September of 2000 while in New York, the same city in which the direction was given to me, I was told that it was now time to write the book. For a moment I asked: what book? Then I quickly remembered the book I was directed to write those many years ago. What these years have given me is knowledge of myself and the process of initiation. This journey of self-knowledge gives one an account of the path of illumination, which is unique to the process. This process of unfoldment opens one up to the source of true knowing which establishes an unbroken connection with he who sent you - the divine essence we call God.

What is revealed in this relationship, are the principles, underlying all life and creation. The knowingness of one's Oneness with all life becomes unequivocal. It is from this place that I come to you as your fellow companion on a journey begun in the distant past. I came to understand that the confusion and pain of humanity has its roots in the loss of memory of his origin, his purpose here and his essential destiny.

What is mostly forgotten is that this experience here on this planet is not a misadventure or the result of a curse or a mishap in the divine plan. To the contrary, humanity with full awareness, made the decision to embark on this adventure. He has forgotten about the brothers and sisters he has left behind on all the numerous star systems scattered throughout the many universes. With this limited memory of self and the past, mankind set about to create limitedness. What we see in manifestation is a result of that creation. The premise on which this adventure was created was to separate out the two aspects of the self - one feminine and one masculine. Mankind set out with the idea that these two aspects were separate and contradictory to each other. This illusionary idea has set up a chain of events resulting in the conflicts between man and woman and all of the other pairs of opposites— rich and poor, black and white, higher and lower and the list extends into infinity. We have created a devil to be responsible for all our acts of separation, ignorance and fears. Conversely, a being called God is then attributed with all the qualities we call "good." This childish thinking has persisted for eons with small groups of souls emerging in each cycle who would penetrate the illusionary veil and merge with the knowledge that evil and good, light and dark were never two separate realities but in fact two aspects of the one thing.

This group has produced the avatars of each round and is responsible for shining the light of truth to the rest of humanity traveling up the mountain path. At the beginning of each major cycle, the idea for that round is seeded in the consciousness of humanity to unfold the next level of consciousness dictated by the divine plan. The middle path on which humanity is now embarking at the beginning of this age requires a mature approach to the ancient issues of good and evil which began this experience into matter. To help elucidate this issue and to bring hope to a wary humanity, I have addressed in this book the fundamental reasons for the conflicts of every kind faced by humanity and offer the solution to lasting peace. The concept of two forces, one evil and one good, attributed to the Devil and God respectively, who are battling for supremacy is the stuff of the childish mind. Now that mankind has come of age, he must put away such thinking. He must dare to face the truth of his own nature and his personal and collective creations.

Every situation and circumstance of life involves our active and our passive participation. It is no longer enough to point the finger. The concept of separation of any kind is what the ancients define as evil and so, no one is without 'sin'. Only when we take responsibility for what has transpired here on earth will we experience the freedom from pain we so desperately seek. No one is coming to save mankind from anything and least of all from himself. He must solve the riddle of the sphinx, which is the riddle of his own life and is none other than relationships or the pairs of opposites. A great difficulty humanity seems to have is the knowledge that he is sovereign and possesses the ability to orchestrate his own liberation from bondage. To him, it is an elusive concept that he can achieve full consciousness and that the achievement of Jesus is his personal goal also. It, therefore, begs the question of what mankind understands as his purpose and journey here in this life to be. After being told repeatedly by Jesus that he was not anyone's savior but a brother and way-shower, humanity still has difficulty acknowledging the high estate of his own heritage.

The idea of being equal with Jesus seems so sacrilegious that he is content to remain in a position of "a lesser being." No master of wisdom finds comfort or receives any pleasure in seeing and watching humanity play small. In fact it brings great sorrow to their hearts because they have come to know through their own unfoldment to self-knowledge, the truth of the divinity of Man. It is in full remembrance, of this fact, that all heaven waits and to which the divine feminine is now ready to prepare humanity to return to full consciousness. Central to this achievement is the correct understanding of the feminine. It is because of the debased position of the feminine aspect of God that life here has been out of balance. Therefore, to achieve peace, prosperity and the manifestation of the divine will to Man, 'water' in all of its aspects must be lifted up. She, the mother, the destroyer, the nurturer, the teacher and the sustainer will be restored to equal power and rulership in the Aquarian Age. She will regain her true position in the minds of men. They will remember the great teacher who took humanity on the adventure of separation to "grow" him in consciousness. This adventure was none other than creating the illusion that good and evil were two opposing concepts. What she did was to create a mental construct whereby the appearance of the negative and positive aspects of life seem to be in conflict and contradiction to each other. She is the woman spoken of in the Book of Revelation who is the keeper of the arcane mysteries. She, we are told, is the keeper of the ancient secrets contained in the book she carries. The revelation of these mysteries contained on her scroll is what is contained in the seven chapters of this book I was asked to write.

I was directed to pull together the essential aspects of these vast bodies of ancient knowledge and to put them together in a comprehensive form. The purpose of this is to make this information, which is essential for the unfoldment in the Aquarian Age, accessible to all who seek it. This is the age in which the occult secrets will be revealed and the correct understanding of man's origin and destiny will be made plain. To this same end, the role that masonry plays in this understanding will be unveiled, since the Masonic legend and story is central to the plan of man's emergence into light over the next 2500 years. The mental and emotional maturity, made possible by the work of education in the Piscean Age we are now leaving, has allowed for the seven disciplines of astronomy, geometry, music, arithmetic, logic, rhetoric and grammar to make the mind expanded and prepared for the revelation of the soul's higher knowledge. This book, *Understanding Your Choice*, so rightly titled, puts humanity at center stage where he belongs. It challenges him to dare to remember who he really is and to take responsibility for the decision he made to embark on this experience.

In the first chapter, he is taken through the twelve signs or divisions of the Wheel of Life to understand how these twelve forces of energy and their attendant impact influenced his physical, emotional and mental development. In every cycle and at every stage of the involutionary process, through the four kingdoms, the goal of preparing the personality vehicle to receive the full in-flow of the soul force has been carefully monitored and supervised. The purpose for this is to restore him to full memory of his godhood.

Chapter two speaks of the descent of consciousness through the ten cosmic centers called Sephiroth and their twenty-two connecting paths to present the glyph of the spiritual man. These thirty-two forces of power represent the cosmic and planetary interplay man enjoys with the stars. Through these forces, he descended into matter through the four worlds to take up residence in matter. The Prodigal Son is used to illustrate this journey, as he went out from his Father's House into the far country and returned with an expanded consciousness.

The story of masonry and the Jewish people, in chapter three, gives the prodigal son a context or framework within which to make meaning of his life experiences. The story helps him to see the analogy they bear to the experiences of his brothers and sisters in every culture and race; to humanity as a whole, to the solar system we inhabit, and the eventual destiny of Man. In the next chapter, the Age of Aquarius— the Age of Occultism— will see the restoration of the

Feminine to her true place of equal power and rulership. The unveiling of the ancient mysteries will bring the understanding so needed for the peace and prosperity so anxiously awaited. However, only when the male-female balance is achieved can this be realized.

In chapter five, the New World Order, so much talked about, is correctly presented. It will be seen that the total administration of this body is under the direction and supervision of the spiritual hierarchy of the planet. Contrary to popular opinion it is this group of souls who have achieved illumination through the steady climb to the mountaintop of initiation who work behind the scenes to impulse those who are in positions of external leadership. They see to the execution of the divine plan as it is revealed to and through them. They have achieved the state of Oneness and are now qualified by their administrative intelligence to lead humanity to true peace and liberation.

In chapter six, titled: Man, the Measure of Things –the revelation of who man is and how he is constituted to reflect the inner secrets he carries within his organism will leave you, the reader, with no other conclusion than that Man is the crowning act of his own creation and that he is in fact God and the sovereign being that he truly is. The seven stages of unfoldment, the final chapter, shows how the aspirant and traveler reverses his journey and walks the path of return consciously toward his full illumination. In these seven stages, he confronts every aspect of himself, and owns all the extremes of good and evil, which have been the sum total of his experiences through his many lifetimes. He now conquers death through the reconciliation of the pairs of opposites and becomes a master of wisdom –never to taste of death again. His travels on the wheel of life are now over and he is free at last.

I invite you to read this book, these living words with attention to detail. Read it slowly, carefully –allow yourself bite-size pieces: chew slowly. Meditate upon and ponder each morsel. Try not to rush to premature conclusions. Allow the soul to reveal itself to you through the deciphering of one line upon another. Let the Divine Feminine, the Way-Shower and reconciler for the Aquarian Age unveil herself to you. She, who is the teacher and the keeper of the hidden secrets of life. Through these pages, She will seed in you the deeper understanding of the choice you made eons ago to come with her on this journey into darkness. She is now ready to lead you out of this illusion of darkness, separation and fear, into LIGHT.

It is my privilege to present this book to you as your servant and companion and to remind you of your ancient home and your inter-connectedness with each other and all life everywhere, in this universe and beyond.

Preface

Etta Jackson's unique gift of getting the kernel-truth in a short sentence shines a light of enjoyment on the writing she has done for her new book, Understanding Your Choice.

The book consists of seven chapters packed tight with information. She reviews in those chapters a number of vast fields of learning. Among others she touches on concepts of metaphysics, religion, masonry and makes them clear to the reader to a degree that demonstrates exemplary writing skills and touches on genius. She also makes the skills useful to the reader's daily life. And she does it so effortlessly there are no creaky encumbrances to stand in the way of her burning desire to give the reader a wealth of wisdom in a very short and intense writing.

Try her book, you'll like it. You will especially like her burning zeal for clarity in brevity. And her skill in including a great amount of knowledge and wisdom in her easy-reading style.

Eugene E. Whitworth, Ph.D., D.OJS

Author of: "Nine Faces of Christ"

"Genesis, The Children of Thoth",

"Eternal Truth", "Jaguar Prince"

48 other working titles

and Poet Laureate of Tarma Province

"Everything is dual; everything has poles; everything has its pair of opposites; like and unlike are the same; opposites are identical in nature but different in degree; extremes meet; all truths are but half-truths; all paradoxes may be reconciled."

The Kybalion by
Three Initiates. p.32

Key 2: The High Priestess

Introduction

"Old things are Passed away, All things are Becoming As New."

The hearts and minds of humanity are now sufficiently opened to be able to feel and to know that there is a link that connects all humanity and all life. This awareness has created a critical moment in the evolution of humanity. Humanity as a whole is now responding to the call from his individual and collective Self, to return to his heritage that is both Royal and Priestly. Under the influence of the planet Uranus that embodies the consciousness of Oneness and is the ruler of this New

Age of Aquarius, mankind is beginning to respond to the urge toward Brotherhood.

For eons, mankind has grappled with the questions of his existence, his destiny, and the questions of: Who Am I? Where Did I Come From? What Am I Here to Do? And Where Am I Going? The struggles to find answers to these questions have led to much contemplation and inquiry by some and a feeling of frustration, hopelessness and being trapped by many others.

The confluence of energies now being emitted into our planet by the Spiritual Hierarchy coupled with the high level of human development is providing a suitable environment for the rigorous investigation to these pressing questions. Humanity is demanding more time for self-discovery and reflection. The more the individual knows of himself and of his environment, the greater the feeling of control over his life and his destiny. To gain that control, it is essential that his understanding of the Causal level of his existence and his reason for embarking on this adventure to Earth be realized.

The search for philosophical and psychological explanations for our existence has brought us to a wonderful and expanded mental and emotional level of development. One that now enables us to sense that there is a significant next step in our evolution. There is emerging a great desire to penetrate into an even deeper understanding of life at its Core, which is to reach above and within to find the Source of this Dance of Life.

All through our history, the more intellectually and spiritually advanced of our race have given us glimpses into the deeper realities, which lie behind and beyond the superficial beliefs and understandings of our present realities. Among these advanced souls are Pythagoras, Plato, Socrates, Francis Bacon and, of course, the elder brother of the

Race of Man and leader of Piscean Age, Yeshua Ben Joseph. He is who we in the West call Jesus the Christ.

There are many schools of thought on the origin of Man. One of these ideologies is the ancient Masonic story acted out in the Masonic rituals. I will speak about Masonry at great length in this volume. It is important to understand the importance of this arcane knowledge and its significance to the Age of Aquarius. In this Age, Masonry will be a restoration of these ancient and sacred Mysteries. It will correctly reflect the expressions of the Soul which are the true intent for which the Great White Lodge on Sirius gave Masonry to Humanity.[1] The distortions we have witnessed over the centuries are also reflective of the distortions of the personality expressed as separateness, exclusion and cruelty.[2] Masonry is a gift to humanity and our destinies are inextricably linked to it.

The story of Masonry tells us that just as the Candidate for initiation enters into the Lodge from outside the Lodge, mankind entered into Planet Earth from outside this planet. Man, a spiritual entity symbolized by a circle, descended from his high estate into Earth, symbolized by the square. Spiritual man entered into the Lodge of Earth to unfold his full divinity while in flesh. This is what has been referred to as the "squaring of the circle." In the Lodge, as on Planet Earth, the candidate subjects himself to graded, disciplined training with definite objectives.[3] The primary objective is self-knowledge and with this knowledge, he has an obligation to be in service to all Life. The long years of intense formal and informal training unfolds in his heart and mind a deep understanding of his own nature and, therefore, the nature of all life and his connection to them. He later begins to extrapolate this knowledge so as to contemplate his connection with life in the solar system, the galaxy, the universe and all life everywhere. The Masonic story is occult in its nature. The word occult has conjured up frightful images in the minds of many who are ignorant of its true meaning. The term will increasingly become commonplace since the Age of Aquarius is the Age of occultism and the externalization of the Western Mysteries. Conversely, we are leaving the Age of Mysticism, which we experienced under the Piscean Age, but we are not leaving its contributions behind. Occultism, which means hidden or secret knowledge was ironically, never hidden since nature lay bare all the so-called hidden mysteries. It was always available for all who were mature enough to "see". The ancients have told us that whatever we are afraid of holds the greatest promise for our liberation. Mankind has tended to be afraid of what he does not understand. To change this pattern, he must seek to know.

In principle, all religions in all cultures have at their core the Masonic blueprint. The form in which it is practiced might be slightly different from culture to culture and reflect the level of consciousness thus far evolved. Over the last fifty years, a large percent of humanity has increasingly expanded his search for the hidden meanings of life. He is also now accepting that his teachings do not reflect the whole truth of his heritage and destiny. It is also true, however, that due to humanity's emotional and mental maturity, he is now better able to understand more. He is now better able to respond to the sensor that is within him to gradually wake up to his true nature.

An examination of the Masonic ritual gives us some clues to the meaning of our life here and helps us answer the great philosophical questions of Life. When the candidate enters the Lodge, he is placed in the Southwest corner, the place of greatest darkness and ignorance. This was also the placement of the Planet in the solar System. The goal then is to move through and around the Lodge to the East by way of the North, where the veiled knowledge, the unknown or mysteries, resides. As the candidate increases in knowledge, wisdom and understanding, he is able to part the veils of illusion and this illumination duly places him in the East of the Lodge, the place of knowledge and Light.

This story of the candidate's journey is analogous to that of man's journey into form, from a place of high estate. It is similarly the story of the prodigal son spoken of in the Bible. He left home and went on a journey into the far country to gain a knowledge he could not acquire if he had stayed at home. Planet Earth is on a similar journey in the Solar System.

For many this idea resonates at the core of their beings because they have never lost the memory and knowledge of their place of origin. Most of our indigenous groups on all the continents have kept intact the knowledge and connection with their ancient home on the Stars. Robert Temple in the Sirius Mystery gives a compelling account of the long history of the Dogon peoples of Mali and their ongoing relationship with the star system Sirius. NASA later confirmed the precise information of the behavior and position of the planet. Zechariah Sitchin, in his book, The Twelfth Planet gave a researched account of the origin of mankind and our eventual destiny. However, Ageless Wisdom has known all this and more for thousands of years. Mankind is being impulsed all the time to wake up out of his long sleep and to re-discover himself and his home. Man's journey into this human experience is the combined effort of three Great constellations: the Great Bear, Sirius and the Pleiades. They represent the Supernal Triangle of God the Father, God the Son, and God the Mother aspect respectively. Qabalistically, they represent Kether, Chokmah and Binah on the Tree of Life. These three forces have influenced our experiment and adventure. Humanity is here to discover how far from the center of light he can travel and still make his way back home safely without losing all memory of his origin and his oneness with his fellow beings and all life. These three energies in a step down process express themselves through the three centers closest to humanity: Shamballah, the Hierarchy and Humanity.

The impulse for this experiment came out of the constellation of the Great Bear, which represents the Primal Will or Divine intent for mankind. It is the center from which the idea for creative manifestation originated. It is the lower level of this Will that humanity calls self-will and it is through the medium of the zodiacal sign of Aries that this experiment was initiated. The seven leading Stars of the Great Bear are said to be that of seven constellations from which the seven planetary influences impact our Earth. These make up the seven Rishis or seven brothers of the Great Bear.[4]

Sirius the "dog star" is said to be the "Great instructor of mankind" from which the governance of this planet is orchestrated by the Lord of Action and Reaction commonly known as Karma. The goal of its leadership is the development of cosmic consciousness on the mental plane. Sirius impacts our planet through the influences of Uranus, Neptune and Saturn to provide the conditions for the reaping of souls that is now taking place. The connection with Sirius is, therefore, being felt by a large number of souls due to the advancement of consciousness that has occurred here on planet Earth. The consciousness of Love-wisdom is the focus of this second member of the great supernal triangle. It is from the great White Lodge on Sirius that the work of the Seventh Ray of Ceremonial Law and Order issues. This energy will produce the conditions that will permit the re-appearance on Earth of the Mysteries of Initiation. It is in this context that Masonry will be reformed, understood and become open. The Sun has veiled the hidden planet Uranus but now employs it as the agent through which it focuses its influence like a lens to externalize the arcane mysteries in this Aquarian Age. The sign of Gemini, the sign of relationships, has provided a portal through which humanity came to experiment with relationships between all pairs of opposites. It is under this sign, and from Sirius that the Masonic tradition was given to mankind.[5] Its distinctive symbols of the two pillars of the temple, one white and one black, offers for our meditation the extremes of relationships. The Hierarchy or the Soul level of expression of our planet is the medium through which the Lords on Sirius work.

The Pleiades, the third aspect of the triangle, is referred to as the seven sisters and the brides of the seven brothers of the Great Bear. It is this union of the seven brides and the seven brothers that the book of Genesis speaks of when it refers to "the sons of God who are gone down to lie with the daughters of men." We place the seven sisters of the Pleiades in the sphere of Binah, the Great Mother and in union with the seven brothers of the Great Bear in the sphere of Chokmah. They gave birth to the Sons of men we call the seven planets: Jupiter, Mars, the physical Sun, Venus, Mercury, the Moon and the Earth. These seven planets express their seven vibrational frequencies or Rays through the seven chakras along the spine to support and nurture physical, emotional, mental and spiritual life on this planet.[6] The Pleiades is situated in the constellation of Taurus, the sign of dense matter and of eventual illumination. Through the influence of Taurus, the aspirant presses on and finally develops the ability to "see". From the cave of this dense matter, the Christ -child is hidden and is later born. The energies of the Pleiades are directly connected with the development of the personality and, therefore, work most closely with the Human Kingdom. The Pleiadean influences later move the aspirant from the Path of Probation to the Path of Accepted Disciple.

These three forces of the Great Bear, Sirius and the Pleiades, working through the Monad or Spirit, Soul and Personality centers, distribute their energies through the twelve signs of the zodiac under the influence of the seven planets. These twelve signs fall into two categories. Seven of these influence the evolution of planetary consciousness on our planet. The other five: Cancer, Leo, Scorpio, Capricorn and Pisces, directly influence the development of the five continents of Europe, Africa, Asia, Australia and America.[7]

The twelve signs can be configured to form three crosses expressing the triplicity and quadruplicity of the zodiac for every perfected soul that must pass through the metamorphosis of the Cross. The elements of Air, Earth, Fire and Water make up the four arms of the Mutable, Fixed and Cardinal crosses. These three crosses represent the crosses that stood on the Mount of Golgotha on which Jesus died.

The four arms of the Mutable Cross are Gemini, Virgo, Sagittarius and Pisces. This cross is called the Whirling Cross, the cross of material change and of the Hidden Christ. Because of its mutable quality it provides the aspirant the fluidity between the pairs of opposites until it takes hold of the soul energy. The infant consciousness of the aspirant is nurtured and provided the opportunity to move from the animal soul to a true aspirant. Symbolically, the Mutable Cross represents the unrepentant thief and the personality development of the disciple. It is in the lower aspect of this Cross that the Nazi chose this symbol as theirs, thereby, expressing at the end of the material cycle of human existence, the false and evil use of matter of which separateness, cruelty and selfishness are key. The whirling "swastika" finally flings the aspirant onto the cross of chosen crucifixion, the Fixed Cross of pledged discipleship.[8]

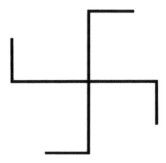

Mutable or Whirling Cross

When the soul has grown in maturity, it mounts the Fixed Cross known as the Cross of the Crucified Christ. The four arms of the Fixed cross are Aquarius, Taurus, Leo and Scorpio. The man who ascends this cross does so by choice and with full knowledge and cognition of the Path he has decided to tread and with all of its implications. He knows that there is no retreat and so he places his feet firmly on the Path of Return. Symbolically the Fixed Cross represents the repentant thief and the Hierarchy or Soul expression.[9]

The Fixed Cross

Having experienced the deaths of the personality and the Soul on the two previous Crosses, the aspirant now ascends the Cross of Spiritual Death upon the four arms of the Cardinal Cross. Libra, Capricorn,

Aries and Cancer takes the now Initiate on to the Endless Way of Revelation. This state of achieved enlightenment marks the beginning of his Cosmic Life of service on the "Higher Way" with all the members of his group. This is the cross of the Risen Christ and all those who stand with the Father at Shamballah.[10]

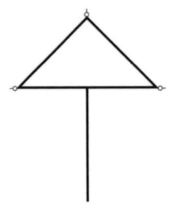

The Cardinal Cross

When the influence of all four arms of each of the three crosses has produced an effect in the disciple, a transition in consciousness is made from one cross to another. Each transition marks a point of crisis in the life of the individual on his Path of Return. The Seven Rays or streams of force conditioned by the seven energies of the Great Bear and the Pleiades give us the astrological framework within which to work out our own salvation.

The travels of humanity through the signs of the sun and all the Stars of the heavens reflect the suffering, triumph and the miracles of the illuminated man before and after Initiation. It is this challenge for the soul to consciously establish the relationship between the divine intent for man's liberation and his physical experience in matter that beckoned us here.

The Emerald Tablet of Hermes

True, without falsehood, certain and most true, that which is above is as that which is below, and that which is below is as that which is above, for the performance of the miracles of the One Thing. And as all things are from One, by the mediation of One, so all things have their birth from this One thing by adaptation. The Sun is its father, the Moon its mother, the Wind carries it in its belly, its nurse is the Earth. This is the father of all perfection, or consummation of the whole world. Its power is integrating, if it be turned into earth.

Thou shalt separate the earth from the fire, the subtle from the gross, suavely, and with great ingenuity. It ascends from earth to heaven and descends again to earth, and receives the power of the superiors and of the inferiors. So hast the glory of the whole world; therefore let all obscurity flee before thee. This is the strong force of all forces, overcoming every subtle and penetrating every solid thing. So the world was created. Hence were all wonderful adaptations, of which this is the manner. Therefore am I called Hermes Trismegistus, having the three parts of the philosophy of the whole world. What I have to tell is completed, concerning the Operation of the Sun.

Chapter One

The Age of Pisces in Review

The Twelve Divisions of the Wheel of Life

Mankind is indeed at the dawning of the Age of Aquarius. He has successfully come through the long night of the last 2,100 years of the Age of Pisces and is simultaneously, completing the almost 26,000year cycle or Cosmic Year, which began in Atlantis long, long ago. Prior to our Atlantean experience, we had journeyed through our Lemurian experience and now we are about to begin the journey of the Middle Pillar. We, the prodigal son, have had our experiences in the far country on the outer reaches of this Solar System and have experienced the extremes of human adventure. The grand lady of the Aquarian Age, Isis herself, welcomes her children home by the light of the Star, Sirius.

The Age of Pisces marks the culmination of the journey which began in Aries, the first Age of the Cosmic Year. It is through the organized and combined influences of the planets in our solar system together with the inner planets or chakras in our bodies that individual and galactic evolution of consciousness is possible. The impact of the combined influences of the three constellations of the Great Bear, Sirius and the Pleiades has brought us to this point of evolution. The seven planets and the twelve zodiacal signs have made this possible. Djwhal Khul in Esoteric Astrology tells us that these three constellations, the Great Bear having the initiating influence, emits the impulses to our Earth through a step down process to Sirius, to the Pleiades and further down to the seven planets. These three constellations are the three aspects of the Trinity or Godhead.[1]

Mankind projects out only one aspect of this trinity for expression and unfoldment at any one cycle. In this cycle, mankind is living out the second aspect of the trinity called the Love-Wisdom aspect. This aspect is under the direct guidance of the planet Sirius. The seven planets are simply seven sub-aspects of this second aspect or Love-Wisdom which mankind is bringing to perfect expression.

The Great Bear or Mother/Father aspect relates to Kether on the Tree of Life, and is the Container of all potentials yet unmanifested. All three constellations are involved in all of the work of the fulfillment of the Divine Will. At this time, however, only the Love-Wisdom aspect has objective rather than subjective expression. The three most recently discovered planets, Pluto, Uranus, and Neptune, are called the outer planets. They are assisting us to refine our vehicles to better facilitate the sequential infusing of light and consciousness. The outer planets have corresponding placements in the human body, along the spine, as energy vortices called chakras, and as the higher octaves of three of the seven primary chakras. Pluto is the higher octave of Mars; Uranus is the higher octave of Mercury; and Neptune is the higher octave of the planet Venus. These three outer planets also correspond to the three constellations of the Great Bear, Sirius and Pleiades, respectively, in the qualities of their energies toward the desired goal - the achievement of "Christ Consciousness."

This capacity for full consciousness caused humanity to enter into the agreement to evolve the Christ consciousness. The elder brother of the race demonstrated this for humanity during his time with us on the planet, over two thousand years ago.

Sirius oversees the second aspect of the trinity, which is responsible for our system of education and religion. The goal is the understanding of the nature of good and evil which are the dual aspects of God and Man. The Great Bear presides over the first aspect of the Godhead, which establishes our governmental, political and legal systems. Through these vehicles, the administration of the Divine Will to man becomes a reality. The third aspect, the Pleiades, administers the financial and business plan associated with the evolution and liberation of humanity.

Humanity is at a unique place in his evolution. This end point of the Age of Pisces presents us with a unique challenge for deep self-reflection. It asks whether or not we have comprehended what the experiences of our many incarnations through the varied educational, racial, social and economic adventures were and are truly all about. This place at which we now find ourselves could be likened to the end of twelve years of basic educational training and preparation provided by our life experiences. Before graduation, it is important that a final test is successfully mastered, to ascertain that the curriculum of each of the past twelve Ages of the cosmic year, have been adequately grasped.

To know what it is that is required of Man to master, we will make a quick review of the essential concepts of all twelve signs of the zodiac which make up the Cosmic Year since this road map is, in fact, the path through which we achieve final liberation.

Pisces is said to be the sign that produces the World Saviors. In this context, the saviors who are to accomplish the work for humanity and the other kingdoms in the Age of Aquarius must come out of the Age of Pisces. We are, therefore, not so much looking for a Savior to appear in the skies as we are looking for and witnessing the birth of hundreds of thousands of members of humanity who have achieved the status of Christ Consciousness, thereby, qualifying themselves as "world saviors." They have achieved liberation, which was made possible by their long, determined and conscious work of spiritual transformation, through the twelve signs of the zodiac.

Aries is the first sign of the zodiac and it rules the head and the function of sight. It is a cardinal sign, is initiating in quality, ruled by the planet Mars and represents the element of Fire. The Sun is exalted or has its highest expression in this sign of Aries.

It is a sign of very potent and strong impulses. These are the qualities needed to begin humanity on his journey. A journey characterized by many successes and apparent failures, which will end in final success when the Aries impulsiveness gives way to balance. This initiating impulse is said esoterically to be the "word" spoken of in Genesis as "sound" uttered into the void.

Aries is said to possess three basic urges. The first is the urge to "begin" things. It symbolizes the urge of mankind to come into form and to begin his long journey through the many stages of development. Aries represents the impulse to begin an adventure. Now that we are at the point where Pisces meets Aries at the cusp of the Aquarian Age, mankind is now again feeling the "urge" for liberation from form.

In the second place is the urge to create both individually and universally. Mankind had the need to create something of his own and so the plane of matter offered the most ideal environment in which to do this. Therefore, he made the choice to come into form to act out his strong creative impulses.

The third is Aries' urge for resurrection. It is this same impulse, which allows humanity to first sense the need for the release from form. He feels the weight of matter as being too much to bear and this feeling causes him to want to roll away the heavy "stone" from the entrance to the sepulcher of his soul, so that he might find liberation.[2]

The sign Taurus marks the next phase of this journey. It is one of the four fixed signs and carries great significance in man's understanding of himself. Taurus is ruled by the planet Venus with the Moon in exaltation and represents the element of Earth. In the outer world, Taurus rules the ears and esoterically, his inner hearing, which is directly related to the inner teacher and to intuition. It requires hearing the inner voice or the voice of the soul if we are to ever achieve illumination.

This impulse or sound from Aries is now turned into Earth so as to be carried out by Taurus, which is said to be the "interpreter of the divine voice." It is also the sign in which the "word becomes flesh" and eventually becomes illumined in form. The Moon, which has its highest expression in the sign of Taurus, is the symbol of matter and has always been associated with agriculture and the "form building" side of life. Through this sign the glory of the divine is to become illumined in matter.

When our human form has been duly consecrated, purified and spiritualized, then the glory and the light of Venus can shine through and the Moon aspect or Matter can truly be exalted. Venus is the symbol of earthly and heavenly love and of both spiritual and carnal desires. It is the influence for the realization of the glorification of spirit in matter.

The placement of the little group of stars called the Pleiades in the constellation of Taurus demonstrates the significant interplay between matter and spirit. Taurus is the symbol of matter and its attractive pull brings matter together. The Pleiades represent the nature of the Soul with its vast expansive quality that moves upon the human form. In man, these two forces co-exist to bring about illumination and the understanding of his experiences in form.[3]

The third phase in the continuation of our cosmic journey is the experience of Gemini in shaping our initial desires. Gemini is called the twin, and is mutable in quality and expression. It is symbolized by the element of air, is ruled by the planet Mercury and has no exaltation. It governs the brain, nervous system, the tongue and the organs of speech. It also governs the hands, which are the instruments through which we gain intelligence by doing.

Castor and Pollux of Greek mythology, the two pillars of Boaz and Joachin in Solomon's Temple, and spirit and matter all represent the pairs of opposites that are symbolic of the sign of Gemini. These seemingly opposing and conflicting forces are the instruments through which an intelligent grasp of the association of things with each other must be achieved. This achievement is essential for the liberation of the mind from the appearance of bondage.

Gemini stands for the relationship or the associative aspects between things and is therefore concerned with intercourse, intercommunication, travel and language. Mercury or Hermes is said to be the messenger of the gods to man and the interpreter of the divine messages to humanity. After Man's Taurus phase, he is immersed in matter and needs a set of guidelines to progress on his evolutionary path by making correct meaning of his experiences. Through the influence of Mercury, mankind experiences the development of language, leading to the development of the concrete mind and later, the higher mind. In the exoteric world, Mercury signifies schools, colleges, teaching, learning, and scientific and literary institutions. On the esoteric level, it signifies thought, understanding, reason, intelligence, intellect, and abstract rather than concrete knowledge through the application of pure reason.[4]

For the spiritual aspirant to grasp the significance of Mercury, he must have a good understanding of the idea, the vision and the impulse that brought him into form in the cycle of Aries. He must be immersed in his own form or Taurus body and have a correct identification with his body. This is necessary for an intelligent grasp of the understanding that matter teaches and that which the gods desire to communicate to man.

Next we come to the cycle of Cancer or the fourth stage in the life of the traveler. It is intimately tied to the human kingdom or the fourth kingdom in nature. Cancer is a water sign ruled by the Moon and Jupiter is exalted here. It is one of the four cardinal signs.

The Moon, we have learned is the mother of form and controls the waters, the tides and periodicity. Form is, therefore, dominant in this sign where the Crab, the exoteric symbol for Cancer, is seen carrying its house on its back, illustrating the relationship of the soul and the body.

The personality vehicle is the house constructed to carry out the soul's operation in physical form. It is here that the duality of form and soul is unified in the physical body. As the aspirant progresses on the path in his many journeys around the zodiac on the wheel of life, the esoteric symbol of the Egyptian Scarab comes to replace the Crab as the symbol of Life; and so also must the personality finally surrender to the soul.

In the sign of Cancer, God symbolically breathed into man's nostrils the breath of Life and man became a living soul.'[5] The sign of Cancer is associated with mass consciousness and is the gateway through which humanity emerged. It is said to be the last of the preparatory signs whether involving the involution of soul into form or the evolution of the aspirant as he struggles out of the human kingdom into the Spiritual or Fifth Kingdom. The influences of this sign are responsible for the formation of the human family, the race, the nation and the family unit.

In Aries, man's mental equipment directs him to fulfill his need as he learns mental control. In Taurus, the sign of desire, he begins to receive his first flash of spiritual light and thus, of purified desires. In Gemini, he grows to appreciate the dual aspects of his nature and understands the increase in his immortality at the expense of his mortality. Life, consciousness and duality came into outward manifestation in the sign of Cancer. It is under Cancer that the individual begins to know there is no personal will. He begins to sense that all manifestations are the result of the urge to build the most perfect personality vehicle for the expression of the One Will.

The fifth sign and the next phase is Leo, which is associated with the element of Fire and is ruled by the Sun with Neptune exalted. The lion, king of the jungle, is the exoteric symbol for the sign of Leo. The heart center is the part of the body ruled by Leo. Esoterically, it is in this sign that the King or the soul begins to assume rulership. The mid-day Sun is the esoteric and exoteric ruler of Leo which is the fire that mankind must endure in preparation for the initiations he must take. His three bodies, physical, emotional and mental, must be fully integrated before he is able to stand before the Door of Initiation. This is aided by the coiled serpent at the base of the spine beginning to unfurl and make its way up the spine. This act gives the aspirant a sense of being his own person and so it is through the sign of Leo that the individualization of the aspirant begins. This stage is essential to self-mastery. Man begins to define himself as a particularized aspect on the One Self. It is under this same sign that later in the progression or evolution of his consciousness the aspirant must surrender his over-identification with the "me" for the good of the whole. This is finally achieved in its polar opposite, Aquarius, the sign of the brotherhood of man.[6]

The consciousness in Leo is the development of sensitivity. First, the individual becomes sensitive to the impact of the environment on him, then sensitivity to the will and finally to the desires, and needs of his lower self. Later, he becomes sensitive to the soul and its needs so that, that portion of the divine plan can be fulfilled through his vehicle. The next level of sensitivity is the fusion of the personality and the soul, which allows him to become an unobstructed vehicle for the expression of the One Will. An understanding of these physical and spiritual sensitivities is the essential state, which must be developed in everyone who walks the Path of Return. Everything has a sun center in its being and so this process applies to all life.

Virgo, the sixth sign, is the next mode of consciousness to be evolved on the path to Christ Consciousness. Mercury is both the ruler and the planet of exaltation in this sign. It is a mutable Earth sign. The action of the soul on the aspirant at the end of his

Leo experience has now fitted him and made him receptive to the impregnation of the divine spark for the "conception" of the Christ consciousness. It is in this sign that the Christ consciousness is conceived and is given birth to in the sign of Pisces, the polar opposite of Virgo, as the world savior. The Tibetan indicates that this sign symbolizes the whole goal of the evolutionary process. Here, in this sign of Virgo the hidden Spirit is shielded, nurtured and finally revealed. Every form hides the spirit but the human form is the best equipped to bring forth the divine intention.[7]

The part of the body ruled by Virgo is the small intestines, the area in which absorption takes place. Esoterically, this is called the "house of bread" or Bethlehem where Christ was conceived of the Virgin Mother, Virgo is a reference to Eve, Isis and Mary, the synthesis of the three aspects of the Mother. Each represents, respectively, the mental, emotional and physical expressions of the divine and hidden presence of spirit in man.

In the aspirant, the process of absorption is an important alchemical process from which the magical substance *chyle*, an extract from food, is released in the blood stream, when the conditions of consciousness are correct. The blood is now charged, which begins the transmutation of the individual from human to God/Man.

The sign of Libra, the seventh phase of this journey through form, is one of the four arms of the cardinal cross. Its ruler is Venus with Saturn in exaltation. One of the attributions of Libra is balance represented by the Scales of Justice. Libra is said to exist between heaven and earth and is, therefore, called the sign of the great interlude. The "Christ child" born in Virgo is said to have gone through an interlude called "the eighteen lost years of Jesus" from 12 to 30 years old. Libra is the sign of clarity gained through the weighing and balancing of everything so as to gain greater insight and understanding. This interlude was taken by Jesus after weighing and balancing spiritual truths with the Rabbis in Jerusalem.

At this stage, the aspirant has developed the ability to know that, in a sense, truth does not really exist and so his quest for the truth ends. Instead, he realizes that all truths are but part of a whole. His energies are now given to the development of discrimination.[8] He is learning the meaning of Justice, Divine Justice.

The impulsiveness, violent fluctuations and exaggerated efforts of the Aries phase, the polar opposite of this sign, reach their point of mental and emotional balance. The lessons of the last five stages of evolution bring the aspirant to a more mature perception of reality. The aspirant is now finally grasping the tenets of the principle of Polarity, which states that, 'all manifested things have two sides with manifold degrees between the two extremes.'[9]

The Scorpio stage and the eighth mode of consciousness is associated with Death. It is co-ruled by Mars and Pluto with Uranus in exaltation. It is one of the four arms of the fixed cross. The Christ child born in Virgo comes of age in the quiet realization of Libra. He has a clearer understanding of the relationship of the pairs of opposites to each other. In this sign, the illusion of separation is shattered by the destructive action of Mars. The aspirant must prove to himself that matter no longer holds dominion over him. Here, the Higher Self is determined to see the death of the little self so that the Soul can more freely express through the vehicle of form. As one of the aspects of the Fixed Cross, Scorpio plays a very important role in preparing the aspirant to enter upon the path of discipleship. Mars' action signifies not only a turning point in the individual's life, but also in humanity. Only when the bodies are sufficiently aligned does Scorpio exert its force.[10]

Scorpio is under the influence of the constellation Sirius, who oversees the initiation of the individual and humanity. In Scorpio, the desires of its polar opposite, Taurus, are transmuted into aspiration, as man turns his direction from matter to the attention of the Soul. Death or change is always the entrance into a more expanded life. If there was no death, the process of evolution could not occur.

The sign of Sagittarius is the ninth phase in the evolution of consciousness. It is influenced by the element of Fire and is one of the four arms of the mutable cross. Its planetary ruler is Jupiter and has no exaltation. The centaur, half-horse and half- man is its symbol. Other symbols are the archer and the eagle in flight. Sagittarius, therefore, is the mode of consciousness that develops in the aspirant, the focused one- pointed nature needed to ascend the mountain in Capricorn.

Jupiter is said to be the planet of expansion that takes us into the far country and to distant places. This sign has been called the sign of "silence." In this silence, the truth of the Path is revealed. The Sagittarian quality in the aspirant allows him to see the goal and with quiet resolve, set out to attain that goal. In this sign, he learns the ability to restrain his speech. He masters the control of his thoughts and develops harmless love.[11] The soul has, therefore, reached the potency of power necessary to enable him to stand before the gates of heaven and hell. His love is born out of the struggles and realizations of his journey. He has developed the capacity for true love, which is one of compassion and true identification with his brother in all the circumstances of their lives.

The sign of Capricorn is one of the most important. It is one of the four arms of the cardinal cross and is one of the three Earth signs. The planet Saturn with Mars in exaltation rules it. The symbol for this sign is the goat with its three aspects; the ram, the scapegoat and the mountain goat. At the bottom of the mountain is Sagittarius, who now clearly sees the goal, which is to climb to the top of the mountain. This is the goal of spiritual attainment or Christ consciousness, achieved in Capricorn by the aspirant.

In its polar opposite of Cancer, mankind came into the kingdom of form, and in Capricorn, he enters into the kingdom of spirit. This is a place in the aspirant's evolution of consciousness where his focus is no longer on the form, but on spirit. He functions through his soul. His personality vehicle is his tool to carry out his service to humanity. It is at this point that the aspirant becomes an initiate. Having reached the mountaintop the aspirant is now free. He has journeyed through nine phases to achieve liberation on the mountain of transfiguration in the tenth sign of Capricorn.[12] In the American Indian mythology, it is said that a baby is born in nine months and ten moons, which is a definite reference to the liberation of the soul out of matter in the sign of Capricorn, the tenth sign. Now a member of the fifth kingdom, the Initiate works as a god/man in a human body. The stages of his development are recorded in the brain of the aspirant and he knows who he is but he remains silent about who he is in the world of humanity. He now descends the mountain of great attainment to begin his work in silence in the valley of humanity with humility and immense love. This is usually called the descent into hell. The initiate will rarely, if ever, admit to anyone who he is.

Under the next two signs Aquarius and Pisces, the initiate embarks on his great universal service to humanity and all life. These initiates will now begin the task for which they gained liberation, to serve his brother, which is humanity.

The sign of Aquarius is the eleventh gate and the doorway of humanity into "heaven." It is one of the four arms of the fixed cross. It is an air sign and is symbolized by Isis holding two vases and pouring water in a pool with one, and with the other, pouring water on the land. It has two planetary rulers, Saturn and Uranus, demonstrating man's evolution out of form into formlessness. Saturn opens the door of opportunity by developing in us the spiritual muscles, the discipline and endurance needed to take us to the end of our journey. These qualities are required to take humanity from darkness into light where the true relationship between spirit and matter is understood.[13]

In the Age of Aquarius, we shall see mankind purified by the living waters and thus, duly purified, he will function more as a soul and less as a human and take his place fully in the fifth kingdom of *homo spiritualis* over the next 2,100 years of the Aquarian Age. In the sign of Leo, the polar opposite of Aquarius, mankind gained his individuality and the knowledge of being a fully evolved human being. He basked in the glory of that realization and saw himself as the center of the universe with the stars revolving around him. However, he began to realize in Scorpio that there was a more expansive world of inclusiveness waiting. This will be the first time in history that the masses of humanity will move onto the Path for higher initiations. This possibility exists because the initiates who are now in embodiment have made the way clear.

In the first decante of Aquarius, we will see the strong influence of Saturn in all departments of life and all the systems of our governments in our world. Saturn, the ruler of the sign of Capricorn, which influences business, will bring about much turmoil in the economic world. Uranus is the planet of spirit and of occultism and transmits knowledge of the hidden mysteries. Its characteristics are the scientific mind, which will aid the disciple in living the occult life and the way of divine knowledge, which will take the place of the mystic way of feeling.[14] The influence of this planet is pulling mankind away from his over-indulgence with matter.

The conflict will be between those who grab and hold for themselves and those who let go to grasp the higher treasures. In this new age we will see all economic, political, racial and physical barriers come down. True respect for each other and all life will be realized. Then, the Aquarian Age motto of brotherhood can be lived out in the "age of the brotherhood of man."

In the eleventh commandment given by Jesus, he said, "a new commandment I give unto you, that you love one another!" With thousands of humans who have taken the major initiations and are now taking their places in service to humanity, many of the issues which have baffled those in authority for centuries will be solved using common sense, a hallmark of the initiate. These souls who now function behind the scenes have been busy laying the groundwork in all departments of the government. Through their work, mankind will see the manifestation of the kingdom of God on Earth. The government of Earth will become the government of heaven as spirit and matter merges.

The twelfth and last sign of the journey is that of Pisces, ruled by both Jupiter and Neptune, with Venus in exaltation. It is one of the four arms of the mutable cross and is symbolized by the two fishes connected by a band. The feet are the part of the body representing this sign. It is in this sign that the World Savior is crucified and the animal nature is transmuted. The Christ has risen and has disappeared for the last two thousand years and on his departure, he assured us that he would re-appear. This is the season for his return according to the signs we have been given. Whether or not he will return in a physical form is largely unimportant. Of greater importance is the state of consciousness to which mankind has evolved. The men and women who have achieved Christ consciousness must now carry out the next phase of humanity's evolution. They are the advance guard for the re-appearance of the Christ.

This is the last of the three signs of salvation, the first being Leo, in which sign mankind is admonished to:"work out thy own salvation." This admonition led to mankind standing on his own two feet to acknowledging his individualism as a human being. Secondly, under the sign Sagittarius, mankind becomes tired of asserting himself and comes to a silent understanding of service to humanity. In Pisces, he carries out the work of the world Savior. The world Savior accomplishes this service by being the connecting link and transmitter of energies from the cosmic kingdom above to the human kingdom.[15] This is the group of souls now in embodiment upon whom the burden of leading humanity has been laid. They go about their tasks with little fuss and with no need for recognition for themselves.

The basic concept to be grasped by the aspirant enabling him to move uncompromisingly onto the Path of Return is the understanding that we are ONE, of the One and from the One. The encouraging news is that everyone will and must come to this point however long it takes and by whatever means his soul uses to get him to this place of understanding. It is on this point that mankind's treatment of his brother will be greatly adjusted and on which the foundations of separation will begin to crumble.

The Age of Pisces began with the advent on the world stage of a personality called Jesus the Christ or Yeshua Ben Joseph. However, during the last two thousand years, in every culture around the world, this same symbolic personality has emerged as the way shower; one who would live out the concepts of the divine plan for humanity, making it easier for each one coming behind to understand the plan. For the

Moslems, we have Mohammed, for the peoples of South America, Quetzacoatl. The Chinese were sent Lao Tse, for the Hindu, Krishna and for the Buddhist, Lord Buddah.

It does appear, therefore, that from a larger worldview, every region of our world is given a similar personality figure that would assist in teaching to humanity that which Divine mind wanted to communicate to humanity. When we remove ourselves from attachment to, and over-identification with, the personalities of the world teachers, we find that the fundamental messages are all similar. Each is presented in a style most appropriate to the orientation and vibrational frequency of each culture and race.

To see how far we have come and how successful we have been, we must start at the beginning by examining the tenets of the messages these teachers delivered. To do that successfully, I believe it is crucial that we look at the sign of Pisces, the last sign of the zodiac, for some of the essential details of the journey.

Pisces is said to rule the feet and symbolizes the fact that in order to have a full grasp of the knowledge of self-mastery, one must walk the journey on his own feet.[16] One cannot stand on the mountain of spiritual attainment without knowing every step on the trail that leads to that mountaintop.

The sign of Pisces, the last sign of the zodiac together with its polar opposite Virgo, is said to be a synthesis of all of the twelve signs. Through their decanates and their respective rulers and exaltations, the sign of Pisces is responsible for preparing the body of humanity for the marriage of his Personality and Soul and in turn, to the Earth Soul.

The alchemical work of the completion of the Great Work through the marriage of the Sun and the Moon with the aid of Mercury can be seen in the work of Pisces and Virgo. Mercury, the ruler of Virgo, is the planet associated with the pineal gland, the organ that reflects the Sun. Pisces, esoterically called the sleep center, is associated with the medulla oblongata, and the pituitary gland or Moon center. Together they carry out the process of the Great Work.

The seven planets of Saturn, Mars, Jupiter, the Sun, Venus, the Moon and Mercury rule these two signs exoterically. The three outer planets of Uranus, Pluto and Neptune also impact the Piscean influence. They are responsible for providing the framework for the body to carry out its work to attain the Great Work, which is that of giving birth to the Christ.

Pisces is thus considered the sign under which intelligence of consciousness is established in the cells. This is the important fourth stage of spiritual unfoldment in the system of Qabalah. It is important to know that one cannot have an adequate understanding of oneself without an understanding of the planets and stars.

The heavenly bodies have a direct impact on our lives since all of these planets and stars reside within our bodies. We are indeed the microcosm of the macrocosm and everything that is outside and above is as that which is below and within. It is for this reason that mankind has been admonished to "Know thy Self." To know one's self is to know the whole universe.

Pisces is directly associated with corporeal Intelligence or body knowledge.[17] The idea being communicated here is that one does not truly know a thing until he has cellular knowledge of it gained through experience. This requires the integrated involvement of the physical, emotional and mental aspects of our being in the process of our knowing.

The Age of Pisces presided over the refining of our body or personality vehicle made up of the physical, emotional and mental bodies. This preparation of the vehicle better facilitates the anchoring of the new and intense frequencies currently being downloaded into our bodily structures. It has been responsible for the evolution of our bodies and its nervous and mental structures for the attainment of full consciousness in the human vehicle.

The alchemical journey taken by humanity is symbolic of the evolution of consciousness achieved through all four kingdoms from mineral to vegetable to animal to human and now, the attainment of humans into the fifth kingdom of homo spiritualis. The fourth kingdom of humans evolved the capacity to reason more rationally and objectively through the ability to see more clearly the relationship and association of one thing to the other in the pair of opposites.

From the concrete to the abstract, mankind has expanded the capacity of his brain and nervous system to receive and house the higher light vibrations coming into his threefold vehicle.[18] The Piscean human began to take the conscious steps to fulfill his long held destiny of unfolding the God he is and was genetically coded to become. These humans are the souls who accepted the challenge to lead the way in coming into embodiment. They began in the crudest of forms, to experience the full spectrum of life in flesh through all the kingdoms. We now have large numbers of fully awakened God/men. They are members of the fifth kingdom and of the office of the Christ who are from every race and creed. They have completed the requisite inner initiations through the extremes of fire and water to understand the inner nature of his God/human self. Mankind is now qualified through his knowledge of the all-encompassing love of all life to serve with God in the liberation of everything in form.

The age of Pisces is also seeing the passing out of the Age of Mysticism and the dawning of the Age of Occultism. We are seeing the struggle of those cultures and personalities who are fighting to hold onto the old way. The sign of Pisces, with its characteristic symbol of two fishes bound together swimming in opposite directions, represents the dualism in Gemini. Each aspect challenges the other and offers enough resistance for growth. The two aspects are merging and as this synthesis surges forward, the illusion of separation is falling away.[19]

The consciousness of separation is ending on our planet as the hearts of humanity open up to embrace the secrets of our common ancestry, heritage and common destiny. Our genetic decoding of the human DNA will uncover the linkages in what Ageless wisdom has always known, that is, we are all One and from the One.

This sign of Pisces brought into form a large number of souls who would play out the drama and meaning of the Age of Pisces. It was important that mankind have the underlying issues of the whole of human evolution projected upon the screen of life. By so doing, we could not deny seeing them and struggle to know their true import.

During the age of Pisces, we have seen some of the bloodiest wars all in the name of God, with real reasons based in materialism, each side proclaiming that he has the correct interpretation of the meaning of truth. Unfortunately, most of the conflict was due to each individual being able to see only his point of view. Therefore, separation became one of the hallmarks of the Age.[20] Some of the characteristics of the sign of Pisces are devotion, idealism to the point of fanaticism, patriotism, and paternalism. Many of our members of this age are desperately trying to hold on to these traditions and beliefs of the past, refusing to give way to a more expansive and inclusive understanding of reality. This struggle to preserve what is no longer useful is causing the pain we are now witnessing globally.

However, as we approach the end of the Age, we have seen an explosion in the education of the masses. No longer is education reserved for a select few. Through education, mankind is learning to liberate himself. He is doing so through his study of logic, mathematics, philosophy, science and the other liberal arts, learning the ability to think and to reason rationally and objectively.

We also saw the birth and extensive use of psychology. Mankind is applying the principles of reason to bring his emotional body under the control of the mind. Humanity is growing less and less ashamed of expressing his emotional pain and disease and is, therefore, now more willing to get the help he needs. Physical, emotional and mental pain is the result of the inability to reconcile the pairs of opposites, whatever they are. Ready or not, the Age of Aquarius is upon us. Spirit is coming down to man and man must rise up to meet it. In the Age of Aquarius, we will see the vision of what God held out for man, when He formulated the idea in Aries, to come into flesh to realize that he is both God and Man.

Table 1: Signs of the Zodiac in Review

Sign	Sign Type	Element	Ruled By	Exalted Planet	Rule
Aries	Cardinal	Fire	Mars	Sun	Head, Sight
Taurus	Mutable	Air	Mercury	None	Brain/ Nervous System, Tongue/ Organs of Speech, Hands
Cancer	Cardinal	Water	Moon	Jupiter	Stomach
Leo	Fixed	Fire	Sun	Neptune	Heart
Virgo	Mutable	Earth	Mercuty	Mercury	Small Intestine

Sign	Sign Type	Element	Ruled By	Exalted Planet	Rule
Libra	Cardinal	Air	Venus	Saturn	Kidneys/Adrenal Glands
Scorpio	Fixed	Water	Mars/ Pluto	Uranus	Reproductive System/ Genitals
Sagittarius	Mutable	Fire	Jupiter	None	Hips/Thighs
Capricorn	Cardinal	Earth	Saturn	Mars	Knees
Aquarius	Fixed	Air	Saturn/ Uranus	None	Blood/ Circulatory System
Pisces	Mutable	Water	Jupiter/ Neptune	Venus	Feet

Chapter Two

The Tree of Life - The Journey of Man

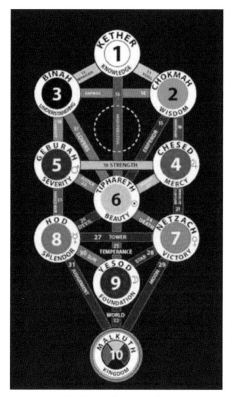

The 32 paths of wisdom

In Earth's early history, mankind made a decision, which would forever change the face of reality on this Planet and the reality of all life everywhere and for all time. Yes, it was a choice, a decision to enter into this journey called life for the purpose of experiencing another dimension of understanding that could only be gained by immersion into form. Under the constellation of Gemini, the Twin, symbolized by the two pillars in the temple of Solomon, mankind made his descent through this gateway.[1] Gemini is ruled by the planet Mercury; it rules the mind and is associated with travel, transportation and inquiry. It is fitting that the principles and vibrational frequency of this sign would provide the right stimulus and conditions for such a journey. At this time in his long journey, it is important for mankind to understand his participation in this planned adventure he agreed to take a long time ago. We have been provided with a guide for our descent into unconsciousness and our eventual return to full consciousness. The religious and philosophical writings of every culture provide ample explanation for that return to the Father. Mankind, however, has been too veiled to remember his decision.

This story of man's adventure is the story of the prodigal son, familiar to many in the west, with similar stories found in every culture. No other story so adequately portrays the story of Mankind's experience from the highest to the lowest point of manifested light.[2] It is important at this point to look at this story in a new light. Mankind has matured enough to begin to remember and take full responsibility for the choices and decisions he made a long time ago. One might ask: how should I be expected to remember what I did all that time ago? The answer is: the vehicle for retrieval is feelings. Every decision, every experience and every adventure you have ever had on this planet or on other planets are etched on your soul as memory. All that is required to retrieve this essential understanding is the willingness to go inside. Using your current pains, ask yourself the right and the hard questions, and the answers will come.

In the following chapters, I will pull together the redemption stories of our many cultures and show how the illusion of separateness has kept man of all races and cultures separated from knowledge of himself and each other. We took ourselves on this adventure to be immersed into matter where we would forget, knowing that we would one day remember. That day is now. The time has now come to remember.

The four philosophical questions mankind is here to answer are:

1. Who am I?
2. Where did I come from?
3. What am I here to do?
4. Where am I going?

Everyone will ask of himself these fundamental questions, because they were encoded in everyone's soul to be pondered at some point along this journey called life.

These were the same self-searching questions the prodigal son asked himself when he reached the extremes of his experiences in the far country. He came to the sobering realization that the foreign land in which he journeyed was not familiar and he needed to go home.

The story of the prodigal son is told in a way that is so simple and is understood by almost everyone. The story of masonry is a little more complex but carries the same message. This story is the story of each individual journey, and the story of the Planet Earth, because the destiny of man, this planet and the solar system are inextricably intertwined.

Each person here is involved in a dance with each other and everything everywhere. We are all sisters and brothers; we are all part of the same WEB of life. When this fact is clearly understood, it should cause each of us to re-evaluate the way we live our lives or this reality called life, together.

The story of the prodigal son begins in the Father's House with his two sons. One day, the younger of the sons, needing to experience life, made the decision to go out from his house. He went to his Father and asked for the portion of money that belonged to him. He did not beg. There was no need to, because he knew he was entitled to it by virtue of his birth. This is the same entitlement that all of mankind is now beginning to understand. This knowledge will allow him to claim his inheritance of the bounties of the Earth!

It is important to understand that he did not leave because he had done something wrong and was thrown out. He left of his own accord because like Buddha, he knew that he could not expand his consciousness beyond his current level of knowing in the environment in which he lived. It takes a measure of awareness for one to realize when it is time to move to the next place, be it physical, emotional or mental.

This courageous young man wanted more. So, he took the portion of wealth, which was his by right of birth, and began the journey that each of us individually and collectively began at the dawn of this cycle of the evolutionary journey. We are continuing to take those journeys throughout the many stages of our evolution.

Under the leadership of the star system Sirius, synonymous with the Father's House, we set off on a journey into matter, also called Maya, to experience what we did not understand about our nature. With each level of decent, we forgot more. It was with the greatest love in our hearts for the idea of expansion of knowledge that we gave up the security of our Home for the sake of experiencing something new to add to the Whole. It was Love that brought us here and it will be Love that will take us HOME. The father loved us enough to not want to hold us back. The father also knew the risks. Every conscious parent knows this, but the Father gave his blessings and said good-bye to his son. He knew that some day he would return and his son would be better off for having taken the journey.

The story indicates that the son took his portion of goods and left. Esoterically we left with the knowledge of our royal birth but as we went further and further down into the abyss of matter, the knowledge of whom and what we really are became more and more obscure and distant. We became amnesic and afraid. The loss of memory developed in us shame, guilt and extreme selfishness. However, that was the Grand Plan from the beginning, to forget the past to become totally aware in the present. How else can one truly immerse oneself into life and gain the full gamut of human experiences unless one has no memory of anything else but his immediate experiences? It worked!! To have no other perspective but the knowledge of what one is experiencing in the moment has profound merit. It allows for knowledge through experience and later, it brings a perspective based on association with a past or similar experience.

No thing can be understood without an association. Later, we can also see that the association of the older brother with the younger brother in the father's house offers this perspective of association. The two pillars in the Temple of Solomon, Light and Dark and all the pairs of opposites of our whole human experience have as their basis the same principles of dualism.

Because mankind, the traveler, needed to go to the end of his human experiences in this far country, at the outer reaches of the galaxy, the cognition to return cannot come until the journeys' end. One of the tools we instituted to help us keep track of our journey and our progress was knowledge of the planets. Their order, cycles, rotations and expressions give us the necessary clues to measure our progress and distance from home. The seven planets, with their definite paths of rotation and seasonal expressions, provide much needed guidance for this young traveler. The elder brother and the Father, who monitored the journey, remained home. The Father was always expectant but had no definite expectations due to the nature of change and its power to transform. The father, however, always knew that his son would not return the immature young man he was when he left.

This young and impulsive traveler used up all of his resources before long. Having no more finances to offer them, all his friends left him. He was forced to resort to eating the pig's food. Since this story is set within the middle-eastern religions and cultures, it may be obvious to see why this would have been the ultimate degradation. Symbolically, this story signifies the fact that mankind has gone to the depths of himself to know and understand himself and his own nature. What has he not done in order to obtain his goal! We embarked on this experiment to experience the two extremes of our nature so that, out of our collective experiences, we may discover the greatest strength that the love of self can offer us.

As a result of this desolation, he comes to himself and makes a definite decision: "I must return to my father's house," as will everyone eventually. He concluded that he could not expect to return to the position he had once occupied. Instead, he would ask his father to be a servant. Similarly, humanity has devalued the knowledge, experience and wisdom he has gained throughout his journeys. The Father, knowing how valuable his son's new knowledge was to the plan of redemption, elevated him to a position above the elder brother who had chosen to remain at home. If we regret our experiences, we regret our acquired knowledge and our much vaster wisdom! The prodigal son is experiencing, at this point, a crisis of conflict. This is one of the seven crises every soul must go through. This test, influenced by the sign of Scorpio, is called the supreme test because it is responsible for man's emancipation from illusion and the freeing of perception from the mists, miasmas, glamour and appearances behind which Reality veils itself. The prodigal son, on "coming to himself" and deciding to return home, passed successfully through his greatest trial and therefore, the nature of his problem changed. He demonstrated his capacity to overcome desire and therefore is no longer taken in by appearances. He can now walk focused and one-pointedly in and toward the Light. He has now become a world worker.[3]

In this New Age, Isis, the lady of the Aquarian Age, will unveil herself to us. In so doing, she will reveal to us the unknown mysteries. She will facilitate the complete opening up of humanity's capacity to understand and remember our true nature and heritage through the most profound language - feeling. That is, we will understand feeling and thus, our minds and our hearts will expand beyond our imagination.

Mankind has had profound emotional experiences with God in the course of his search for answers to the four fundamental questions. He has listened to theologians trying to explain God and has felt a measure of the knowledge expressed, but there is an increasing need to apply his own interpretation to what he has experienced. There is also a yearning in many to understand the deeper meaning of life and truths that might lie beneath them. The new generation has challenged the older generation to revisit their explanations of life's perplexing issues. The new have dared the old, leading by example, to pry open those premises they regarded as sacrosanct.

The Aquarian Age is the age in which the deep mysteries and secrets of Pisces will be unveiled as Isis unveils herself to those whom she finds worthy. The great so-called mysteries of life are not really mysterious at all. What is required is the willingness to see. To those, and there will be many, who have become tired of closing their minds to what feels uncomfortable, these new times offer a most exalted opportunity. For many, the search for the Ancient knowledge will bring them to a study of the Ageless teachings of wisdom. That investigation will invariably bring every true searcher to study, in some form, the Qabalah. In the distant past, when man was aware of what he might need for his liberation, he developed a body of knowledge to help him on his return. The Tree of Life is a glyph of Man and the container of all that was, is and ever will be. In his long journey, he lost awareness of his knowing; but at no time in the history of the quest for knowledge was there ever an absence of knowledge.

The Tree of Life, the Glyph of man, the planet and the solar system are the Trestleboard on which man marked out the path of involution into matter and his eventual path of return to his home. The place from which this descent begins is the highest point of consciousness held at that time. The Tree of Life is a map of the involution and evolution of consciousness and the Key to man's liberation. Like any conscientious traveler, Man sets his intention on where he wants to go and then proceeds to find the most efficient way of getting there. He also needs to determine what he would like to see and experience along the way. The Pathway consists of passing through many planetary systems that correspond to the different kinds of experiences germane to the Soul's development. For these reasons, a carefully designed blueprint was constructed. This map, and the constructor of the map, are one and the same. The map is an externalization of man's ideas of himself and of his desire to experience himself in the dimension of form.

To set the stage for this journey, it is important to understand the nature of this force or Primal Fire that all the ancients have used to symbolize the initial idea in the mind of the traveler. It is a diagram of the progressive stages in man's mastery of fire and shows the various relationships among the forms in which the One Fire manifests itself. Hidden behind the veiled Light are the limitless possibilities of how the journey is experienced.

The Tree of Life is a diagram consisting of ten spheres numbering one to ten with twenty-two connecting Paths or channels. The Paths are set out in a definite geometric pattern to portray the exact form, measurement and scale appropriate to the precise outcome held by the primal force. The ten spheres are called Sephiroth or emanations of that One Force which we call God and, at the same time, Man. For many, it will seem sacrilegious to imagine or to perceive yourself as the architect or builder of your entire world, but you are. In this new age, we will become increasingly bold in taking our rightful place in the whole scheme of life by taking responsibility for our divinity and sovereignty.

The essential purpose for the study of the tree of life is not the investigation of some external force or being. It begs the contemplation of one's origin and purpose, and correspondingly, of the grid of his own form - the solar system and galaxy in which we live. The questions that will bring anyone to this level of search is the need to know, once and for all, the answers to the four core (p. 37) questions that everyone will ask at some point in life. When man can no longer live with these nagging questions, the desire becomes so strong that he will be driven to take the journey inward to discover for a fact "I and the Father are one. God is Man and Man is God!"

The thirty-two paths on the Tree of Life are synonymous with the thirty-two degrees of Masonry. Everyone must walk these on the journey to liberation in life. Man is just not conscious of what his life is all about. In reality, this Path is about waking up out of this dream, and realizing that the dream and the dreamer are one. That the events of his life mark out the paths, which are set out on his own tree of life. The tree of life, as the glyph of man, contains and is contained within the four worlds of fire, water, air and earth or the worlds of Thought, Feeling, Mind and the Physical.

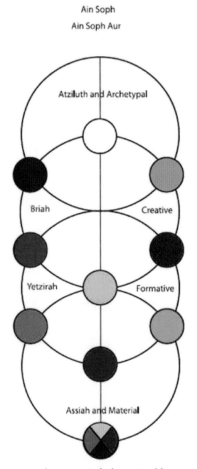

Ain
Ain Soph
Ain Soph Aur

Atziluth and Archetypal

Briah   Creative

Yetzirah   Formative

Assiah and Material

The Four Qabalistic Worlds

The sphere at the top of the tree is called Kether or Crown and is numbered one. It represents the first outward expression of Primal Will. Before anything is seen in the manifest world, there exists always behind it a thought, whether or not man is conscious or aware of that fact. In ageless wisdom, it is what existed behind the veil. The three aspects of thought are referred to as Ain, the "no thing." It is the undifferentiated aspect of Limitless Light or Primal Darkness, the state that everyone occupies before bringing anything into visible expression. Remember, this is all about each individual![4]

The next phase in this step-down process of externalization is the Ain Soph or boundless, limitless, and never-ending whirling energy of thought. This energy or force begins to move in a specific direction in response to a word, sound or note in some part of the universe. This force is searching to find a reflection of itself in form. Thus, the adventure and man's search for himself begins! The only one who knows what he is going after is himself. He is always in search of himself and that knowledge which is encoded in his own being. All of life propels us toward the apparent unknown.

The third phase of the process is termed the Ain Soph Aur. The Light in this phase of its expression, though boundless, contains the potential for what it is to fulfill in all four worlds. In a whirling motion, Primal energy moved out into the manifested form.

The sphere called Kether is the first time we are able to see any evidence of what had gone on before, as is the case with all of our creations. The number designated to it, the number one, is the beginning or initiator of all that follows and represents the first comprehensible idea the human mind is able to formulate concerning the Life Power. It is inherent in man to be able to reason out his relationship to this One Life. This is the conscious or unconscious goal of all Life. The department in which Kether exists is called Atziluth and corresponds with the element of Fire. It is this fire in the head where ideas are formulated for what one wants to create. Nothing is created in the universe or the world unless there is a need for its presence. Think on this! There are no mistakes! Mankind chose to create in form to give himself the ability to touch, taste and feel his own creation. He wanted his experiences to be as tangible as possible and so he continued on his journey to create more mass. The clear intention to embark on this journey is essential because the intent provides the momentum needed to go the full distance.[5]

Chokmah, is the second sphere on the tree or the number Two, which in essence is male but in expression, female. It is the Divine Masculine Principle and is electric in nature. Chokmah is called the Sphere of the fixed Stars, which refers to the knowledge that man carries within himself regarding the connection between the heavenly bodies and the affairs of his life. Chokmah is also called the sphere of Wisdom and is perfect self-knowledge; it knows all its qualities and possibilities. This knowing is forceful, energetic and dynamic, and is the root of all expressions of Life and consciousness.

By branching out, but not separating from, the Life Power extends itself from the point of Chokmah by projecting its essence out through a line called the secret path of the Empress. This sphere, numbered three, is the Divine Feminine Principle called Binah. It establishes, via this line of force, the Empress, the other pole or pillar together with Chokmah that establishes the two pillars in Solomon's temple.[6]

Binah is objectively male but in essence, female, and is the active agency of manifestation. It is considered the root of Understanding and Active Intelligence. In this sphere is concentrated the power of "separation", the ability to tell one thing from the other. It is also related to the knowledge of what supports a concept and is the mental power that gives differentiation, form and substance to all things. It is magnetic in nature and in contrast to Chokmah, it is the power of the One Mind in us that looks toward the center to discern the potentials or possibilities of Being. Binah is the turning of inner consciousness to the outer limits of the fields of manifestation.

Binah is called the sphere of Saturn and is the cause of the many appearances of Name and Form. She constitutes the complex tapestry of apparent existence. This mode of consciousness defines, sets limits and boundaries and specializes. Binah, the Divine Mother, is synonymous with the Great Void and the Womb from which all life came. The color of this sphere is indigo or blue-black. The habitation of God is thick darkness for behind all veils of appearance is the untouchable Divine Glory…darkness is Light that the veiled is unable to behold![7]

Chokmah and Binah are the true parents of mankind and all life. When this parentage is rightly understood, the honor to parents spoken of in the scriptures will be more accurately and comprehensively expressed. Kether, Chokmah and Binah constitute the administrative aspect of the Tree of Life and the three essential aspects of the individuality of God/Man. Kether, the indivisible ONE SELF that is the core of reality within all manifested selves, cannot be divided. Kether represents God as HE is and all things are contained in this ONE. Chokmah, the second aspect of the ONE, is God as He knows himself perfectly and is designated the Masculine or the Father Principle. From that perfect knowledge, is the intuitive perception of what it knows itself to be and from that knowing, establishes itself as the third aspect of Deity that is Binah, called Understanding. This Supernal Triad makes up the human individuality or what is called Super-consciousness and should not be confused with the personality.

Binah creates a vehicle for the expression of this ONE Life in form. The next sphere or the container for the intelligence into form is Chesed, the fourth sphere on the Tree and reflects Chokmah. It receives and arrests the consciousness pouring down from Binah. Measurement and order are therefore appropriately assigned to this sphere. Mercy, majesty and magnificence, measurement and memory are also attributes of this sphere in which the planet Jupiter expresses. All the filing systems and all other mechanical memories in technology and computers, including organization in human life, are influenced by this mode of consciousness. As above so below!

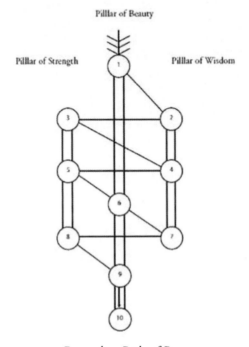

Descending Paths of Power

All of creation is a result of the perfect memory that the One Life has of itself and every event in the series of its self-expression. This is reflected in the orderly development in the course of evolution. Human memory is only one phase of this cosmic memory and nothing is beyond recall.[8]

Geburah, Severity, Strength and Justice are all terms used to describe this fifth Sephirah that is the polar opposite of Chesed, and the reflection of Binah on the Tree. It is termed volition and is aimed at affecting change and transformation. Geburah takes the memory of Chesed and puts it into action. Volition, expressed as will, is not personal but the will of the One Self. The One Self sends every human being into manifestation. There is no personal will and the wise of all ages know this truth. Under this influence is justice and true rule of law established. Just regulation is real law and just volition is true will. Any law that disregards the rights of others is delusionary. Mars, the planet associated with Geburah is a destructive and regenerative force, which is active in all the affairs of life and is responsible for the tearing down of outworn, outmoded, erroneous ways of thinking. When most people have these destructive experiences, the tendency is to feel that they are under attack from some malevolent force. The pentagram or five-sided symbol is that of Man in his right relationship of God to Man and in turn, Man to Nature. I will illustrate that the pentagram is man, the Cosmic Fire, in dominion over nature and more importantly, his own nature of spirit in dominion over matter - air, earth, fire and water. [9] This Man is Tiphareth, the Stable Intelligence.

Tiphareth or Beauty is the sixth Sephirah on the Tree of Life and sits in the heart of the Tree. It is the perfect reflection of Kether and completes the Triad with Geburah and Chesed to form the Egoic triangle of the Higher Soul. Tiphareth is the Archetypal Adam who is the Son of the Father centered in the heart of all life. Tiphareth receives the influence of the energies from above to rule in the kingdom below because it is the active manifestation of the principle of rulership. In Tiphareth, man becomes conscious of his Godhood and realizes the non-existent difference between the "Father" and the "Son". This is Adam or the prodigal Son who left the father's house on his journey into the far country.[10]

The six pointed star or Solomon's seal is the symbol Tiphareth represents. It symbolizes the perfect union of Spirit and Matter and all the apparent pairs of opposites shown on the Tree of Life by the fact that all Paths above and below flow into and from Tiphareth.

Netzach, the seventh Sephirah, is the first of the next four Sephiroth below Tiphareth that forms the personality vehicle. Netzach is called Victory, Occult or Hidden Intelligence and represents the emotional body of the personality. It relates to the "eye of understanding" seen on the dollar bill of the United States and is the all-seeing eye of the Freemasonry symbol. The illumined know that this hidden intelligence is the Primal Fire or Intelligence that operates in all Life. This intelligence knows no failure and no death, just the appearance of it. The One Life cannot fail and every perception of failure is an illusion. How one is able to direct and manipulate the forces coming into one's sphere of influence determines his experience of victory. Netzach relates to the biblical passage; "He will swallow up death in victory," or victory over the illusion of failure.[11]

Hod, called Splendor, is the eighth sphere on the Tree and the polar opposite of Netzach. It is the Sphere of Mercury and the Cosmic Intellect. It represents the logical consequence of what was learnt in Netzach. Hod is the combined will-force from Geburah, the image-making power of the Higher Soul and the desire-force in Netzach. Together they establish the intellectual operations of human consciousness. The eighth Sephirah is the Life power's manifestation that is eternally moving from glory to glory. The illumined intellect understands the necessity of sorrow and why suffering is no real contradiction to the idea that the universe is an ever progressive and successful process. This sphere hints at the importance of the mind in the work of Hermes or Mercury in the application of geometry to the science of Masonry. This sphere of consciousness is used in the building of the temple not made with hands undertaken by Hiram Abiff. The analytical nature of the intellect, with its ability to tear things apart - to make logical, rational and objective conclusions, is the quality of Higher Mind.[12]

Yesod is the ninth Sephirah on the Tree of Life and is called Basis or Foundation, the Intelligence of Probation or Trial, and Natural Intelligence. In this sphere, the nature of all things, find full expression and balance. It is where man comes to that place where he desires liberation. No one can achieve adeptship unless he desires it. He must engage his will by way of his decision, and the Life Power must have a fit instrument on which to work. We can then move forward in the confidence that Yesod will carry out what we planned. Yesod relates to reproduction and is the point on the Tree of Life corresponding to the procreative organs of the Adam Qadmon or the Grand Man. In modern psychology, it is designated as the unconscious, subconscious or subliminal consciousness. The power at work in this Sphere originated in Tiphareth and reflects its Solar Light as the Moon reflects the Light of the Sun. Purified Intelligence is applied to this path to indicate that reproductive functions are not evil, as many perceive them. Instead, they play a Key role in the evolution of consciousness on subconscious levels. In this sphere, the masculine and feminine powers come into perfect balance.[13]

Malkuth called the Kingdom, Resplendent Intelligence and the Bride, is the tenth path on the Tree of Life. It is the fruit of the Tree as Kether is the root of the tree. This is the sphere of the physical world that is the seat of sensation and the physical body. Here is the field in which the basic unit of cosmic substance appears to be separated out into the four classifications as: Fire, Water, Air and Earth. The russet segment corresponds to the element of Fire, olive the element of Water, citrine - the element of Air, and black - the element of Earth.

Malkuth is also described as the Bride alluding to and representing the sum total of ALL the influences shown on the Tree of Life. This concentration of influences in the field of manifestation we call the

World. It is this body of mental impressions and sensory experiences that form the basis for human knowledge, accurate or inaccurate.

When we can see the Unity of ALL, we see with an illumined mind. We are then able to see that the real substance of the universe is spiritual. We come to know that what we experience through sensation is the true presence of the Divine Life veiled by the appearance of matter. Malkuth, the fruit of the tree, holds the seeds of new manifestations. This attests to the eternal continuity of all life that has no beginning and no end.[14]

This journey of consciousness through the ten expressions of the One Power is the descent or involution into Form. The Path of Return or evolution requires conscious remembering. Next, we will look at the twenty-two hidden or secret paths connecting the ten Sephiroth.

The Fool or the number Zero is the secret path connecting Kether to Chokmah or Divine Will to Wisdom. He is about to take His plunge into form and he is not afraid. He is the prodigal son and carries in his pouch and on his being all that is needed to sustain him on his long journey. He also represents the innate sense in all of us, the adventurer, that desire to experience more livingness. He symbolizes the projection of the Limitless Light or Life Power out into Time and Space while at all times being the container of the All that is the Life Power. He, the Fool, represents the "I AM" and is that mode of consciousness in man that allows him to see far beyond the seemingly limiting circumstances of his immediate experiences.[15]

The Magician, symbolized by the number One, is the twelfth path on the Tree of Life that connects Kether with Binah and is represented by the Planet Mercury. It is the Sun of our Solar system and thus reflects into form, the Will of the One Life. This path, which connects Kether with Binah also connects Divine Will with Understanding. It represents the initiating steps of bringing the seed ideas of limitless possibilities into manifestation. On the level of humanity, this requires clear, objective, rational ideas about desire. This sharp, focused energy is required to penetrate the field of subconscious symbolized by the next path. The center in the human body associated with Mercury or the Magician is the pineal gland located in the brain. Combined with self-consciousness, it is the ability to formulate ideas.[16]

The High Priestess or subconsciousness is the thirteenth path on the Tree of Life and is the field in which the Magician plants the seed ideas he develops. She is assigned the number Two. The ability of subsconciousness to successfully develop these seed ideas is based on her perfect record and memory of the Life Power's Will and intent for all Life. She connects Kether to Tiphareth or the One Will to Beauty. Subconsciousness is controlled by the pituitary gland in the human body and is known by the masters of ancient wisdom to be the transmitting station through which the mental states of self-consciousness are relayed to the nervous system below the brain. The High Priestess, with her powers of deductive reasoning and perfect memory, carries the responsibility of our personal experiences. It is this mode of consciousness that represents the all-inclusive nature of universal subconsciousness. The pituitary gland or the Moon center and master gland of the body has the collective responsibility for the function of the whole body through the whole endocrine system. It is she who is the representation in Man, of Life and the Unity of Matter and Spirit.[17]

The Empress or the fourteenth path on the Tree of Life is associated with planet Venus and reflects another aspect of the feminine energy. She is assigned the number Three and the attribution of Creative Intelligence. She represents the Great Mother pregnant with the world of form and connects Chokmah to Binah or Wisdom to Understanding.

She is the High Priestess, no longer a virgin, who is impregnated by the Magician with the seed ideas for limitless possibilities in form. She is the wise woman who can only become so by no longer being innocent. She sits in a garden that symbolizes universal subconscious. She, Venus, rules the throat center in the body also called one's power center. Creative Imagination requires that the self- conscious or mental aspect of the self develop the clear, sharp, accurate images wanted in the subconscious. Whatever is planted there is grown successfully by subconscious. The Empress carries a sceptre and wears a crown, symbolic of her dominion and power. She also symbolizes fertility, love, beauty and abundance. It is she who provides for ALL her children in all four kingdoms.[18]

The Emperor is the consort of the Empress and is the next expression of the Magician that connects Wisdom to Beauty. He represents the fifteenth path on the Tree of Life and is ruled by the Planet Mars to which the number Four is assigned. Order, sight and reason are characteristic of the Emperor. He sets order over his kingdom, made possible by the offspring that the Empress produces. Without her he would have nothing to rule over. He represents the mode of consciousness in all of us that is able to see clearly by applying reason based on objective facts. He knows what he has created in his world and takes full responsibility for his creation. Imagination is a key aspect of sight and supervision. The ability to see things as they really are and not how they appear constitutes Higher Vision. This clear vision stimulates the subconscious to produce right outcomes.[19]

The Hierophant represents the sixteenth path on the Tree of Life and is influenced by the planet Venus. He is the next phase in expression of consciousness symbolized by the Emperor and connects Wisdom to Mercy. The Emperor and the Hierophant are not two separate persons. They are one. The Emperor wears the armor and the Hierophant wears the peaceful vestments of his office as ruler of the inner kingdom. The sense of hearing is assigned to him. He hears the inner truth of the One Life with its multitude of applications. He represents intuition, which is reason taken to the next level. He represents that mode of consciousness in all of us who is the revealer of mysteries. However, one cannot hear the Higher Self without the ability to reason and to see things clearly, neither can one be a poor listener and hope to hear the Voice of the Hierophant we call the Inner Teacher.[20]

The Lovers represent the seventeenth path, the number Six and the mode of consciousness called discrimination. The sense of smell and the sign of Gemini are also assigned to this Path. The planet Mercury is associated with this path, which connects Understanding to Beauty. The Lovers is depicted with a man or self-consciousness and a woman or sub-consciousness standing beside each other as the two poles of human mentality. Archangel Raphael, the aspect of super-consciousness associated with Air, is above them and is said to be Hermes or Thoth. This Archangel of healing rules this cardinal point of Air, and oversees the eastern quarter of the heavens. The number six means reciprocity and is the act of giving and receiving and when in harmony, expresses itself as love. Discrimination is the ability in us to perceive the difference between what is real and unreal and requires careful observation. This can only be achieved by an accurate classification of differences as no single event can be properly assessed outside its relationship to its surrounding circumstances. These seemingly opposing poles are two aspects of the same thing and the Unity of ALL.[21]

The eighteenth path is assigned to the Chariot and is called Receptivity. It connects Binah to Severity on the Tree and represents the sign of Cancer, the number seven and is ruled by the Moon. It is related to the mode of consciousness called "The One Will." The two sphinxes represent the opposing forces with the Rider as the reconciling force between them. It demonstrates the question of free will and shows that there is no "free will" -- that all apparent expressions of such are different modes of the One Will. The Chariot is a summation of all the concepts previously expressed. The One Self is the rider in the vehicle of the personality symbolized by the Chariot. When the personality is developed, the mind is able to grasp and interpret the Divine intent streaming through the field of personality.[22]

The nineteenth path connects Mercy to Severity on the Tree of Life and is called Strength; it is ruled by the Sun and represents the sense of taste. A garland of roses, in the form of a figure eight, connects the woman with the red lion or Mars force that she tames. She, like all the female figures on the tree of life, represents different aspects of the feminine principle Binah. Man is the most evolved of all four kingdoms and represents super-consciousness to the three kingdoms below him. Strength demonstrates the immortality of man because, by the mastery of sub-human powers, man is able to achieve liberation and conscious awareness of immortality. 'Until the individual becomes wise enough to select and digest the proper sorts of mental food, he is not ready to experiment with the higher laws of control which enable (sic) adepts to perform their mighty works.'[23]

The twentieth path on the Tree of Life called the Hermit connects Mercy with Beauty. The sign of Virgo, the planet Mercury and the number nine are all attributed to this path. He represents the Response of Matter to Spirit or Man to the One Life. The six-pointed star in the lantern of the Hermit symbolizes the perfect union of "touch", which is the goal of all mankind, however, unconscious he may be of this fact. 'This touch is the union with the Supreme Self. It is intensely blissful and is often compared to the intense physical ecstasy of the sex embrace in occult writings.' The Hermit is the one who holds the lantern and he is also the Light that shines from the lantern that he holds atop the mountain. This is the mountain of spiritual ascent attained in his long climb and he now holds the Light for his fellow travelers still in darkness and coming up behind him. His only concern is that his Light shines bright enough for those who still travel. The reward of his benevolence is not that he is liked but that he radiates the Light of Love. His gray robe is evidence that he has found the balance between the pairs of opposite. He is Hiram Abiff, the Master Mason of the Masonic legend. The Hermit should remind us that we exist because it is the Desire of the One Life. The number nine represents the end of a cycle and thus sets the stage for the beginning of the next phase in the expression of Life.[24]

The number ten, or the number one when reduced, marks the beginning of the next phase of the Fool's journey. It is the twenty-first path called the Wheel of Fortune and is ruled by the planet Jupiter. This path connects Mercy with Victory. The number ten has a direct relationship to Malkuth and the tenth sphere on the Tree of Life. It reminds us that the physical plane is the place where the One Life came to gain full consciousness clothed in flesh. The ability to grasp the understanding of the ebbs and flows of each cycle of evolution is the reward of this path. For this understanding to have practical application, one must be able to flow with the rhythms of nature. The change of the seasons, the periods of light and dark and of contraction and expansion should give us a deeper understanding of our own nature and our link with all life.[25]

The number eleven and the sign of Libra are assigned to the twenty-second path called Justice that is ruled by the planet Venus. This path is called "the faithful intelligence" and connects Severity to Beauty and symbolizes balance. To arrive at a just conclusion, one must be able to weigh one thing against another, having an adequate grasp of the divine laws. Application of justice requires that we first become aware of what needs changing in our own thinking, feeling and desires. According to occult knowledge, the Libra center in the body is connected to the kidneys, and more specifically to the adrenals. They are responsible for emotional balance, the tone of the muscles and more harmonious living. Our fate is determined by the decisions we make, and the subsequent actions we take. As our understanding of the laws of the One Reality increases, we will know truly that justice is the balancing of the scales of action and reaction.[26]

The twenty-third path is assigned to the Hanged Man, ruled by Neptune, the number twelve, and is the root of water. This path connects Severity with Splendor on the tree of life and is called "the Stable Intelligence." The Hanged Man represents one of the three most recently discovered outer planets. His stability and sense of security are not determined by his material possessions, such as where he lives or what he has. His life seem uncomfortable to those looking on. His is a life lived in complete reversal to social consciousness. Contrary to appearances, the Hanged Man is at peace and quite comfortable because his stability is in his individuality. Because of his training, he can give himself over safely to the waters of primal substance. He knows that his support and sustenance comes from the One Self within. He represents that mode of consciousness inherent in all of us, the "stable intelligence."[27]

The twenty-fourth path is assigned to Death, the sign of Scorpio, the number thirteen and is influenced by the planets Mars, Pluto and Uranus. This path connects Beauty with Victory on the Tree. Death symbolizes the destructive action of the Mars forces in the field of personality. Fear of death is one of mankind's greatest fears. Imaginative intelligence describes this path because it is our images that are responsible for most of what we experience. If there were no death, there would be no evolution. The Mars force is the impulse that tears down outworn, outmoded and erroneous modes of consciousness, so that new "life" can begin. Death is not the cessation of life, but transformation and change. The beginning of life is in the seed of life, which comes from the fruit of our experiences. Physiologically, we die daily and the field of medicine tells us that we are continually being reborn.[28] Ageless Wisdom had always known much of what science is now discovering.

Temperance is the name given to the twenty-fifth path that is ruled by the planet Jupiter and is assigned the number fourteen. It represents the sign of Sagittarius and connects Beauty to Foundation. The Archangel Michael rules this line of force, which represents the cardinal point of Fire and the direction, South. It is the path representing the mode of consciousness called verification through probation and trial. The archangel verifies that what we say we know and who we say we are, is tested through the fire of purification and purgation. These are the three types of tests, also taken by Yeshua-Ben-Joseph and which every initiate must successfully pass. They are:

1. The hunger for material objects;

2. Spiritual pride; and;

3. How one uses power in his sphere of influence.

These tests verify the level of development of the personality. The dross of our personality must be burned out so that we become as pure as gold. Only through a focused and pointed goal, symbolized by the archer, can membership in the fifth kingdom be achieved.[29]

Path twenty-six is assigned to the Devil, the number fifteen, is ruled by the planet Saturn and connects Beauty with Splendor. Archangel Ariel stands upon this line of influence in the cardinal point of Earth in the direction, North. He is one of the most important and misunderstood of all expressions of energy. His appearance represents all the fears created by our own thinking and is symbolized by the inverted pentagram on his forehead. It is evidence of the distortion in the way we reason. Faulty reasoning produces "devilish" outcomes. Mankind, the creator of his reality, has convinced himself that he is helpless to change the circumstances of his life. He then attributes his pain to a force outside himself that he feels he has no power to control. A reversal of the process used to create unwanted outcomes, necessitates putting the mind in right relation to divine law in order to achieve more harmonious results. When this happens, he finds renewal that usually comes out of the depth of his sorrow, pain and fears. From some of our deepest agony we seek something better. The divine intelligence rooted in the One Will works through all life to bring each individual "Home". This is the point in the journey of the prodigal son when "he came to himself." It is a place where every member of the human family must come to on his long journey to the father's house. Everyone is destined to make it home![30]

The twenty-seventh path is called the Tower and embodies the planetary force of Mars. It connects Victory with Hod, rules the mind, is phallic in symbolism and is assigned the number sixteen. The tower is a reference to "the tower of Babel" mentioned in the bible. This tower was built to assist in reaching God who was thought to dwell somewhere "up there" outside the realm of the physical. Mankind continues to build his towers of isolation and separation and in this darkness he wonders why he is so alone. The notion of separation gives us the believe that the above and the below, the within and the without, the dark and the light, and all the pairs of opposites have no connection with each other. It is this form of ignorance that is responsible for all the pain and suffering we individually and collectively experience on this plane. The One Life cannot be separated from Itself or we would all cease to exist. Everything and everyone is an aspect of one's self on all four levels of expression. The mode of consciousness assigned to this path is "Awakening." It is only when the individual comes to that point of illumination, when the lightening bolt from the east strikes "his head", that the mind is changed. We cannot give birth to a new reality until the destructive force of Mars tears down the false premises on which our towers are built, at the very foundation.[31]

The twenty-eighth path is that of the Star and represents the sign of Aquarius, ruled by both Saturn and Uranus. It is assigned the number seventeen of the twenty-two secret paths. It is the calm after the storm of the previous path. The mode of consciousness expressed by this path is Meditation. Occult mediation is focused concentrated attention on what one seeks answers to. The central figure on this path is "Isis." She says simply, "if I find you worthy, I will unveil myself to you", "I will meditate you". What prepares one for meditation then is the work with the Mars force at work in the paths of "Death" and the "Tower". A state of receptivity is required. The symbolic cup of the personality must be emptied of erroneous notions about the One Reality. Aquarius is called the "Age of the Brotherhood of Man" and in this new age, mankind will increasingly understand his link with all other humans and all life, at the molecular level of his being. Isis, in another expression of the feminine principle, holds the scroll that contains the laws governing all life. True peace, on the individual, national and international levels can only be achieved by a knowledge and application of the Laws of Life.[32]

The twenty-ninth path on the Tree of Life called the Moon, is assigned the number eighteen and is influenced by the planets Jupiter and Neptune. The mode of consciousness called corporeal intelligence is assigned to this path and connects Victory with the kingdom in Malkuth. This subconscious influence holds the memory of what man is to become. This path illustrates the journey of the One Life through the various stages of evolution, from mineral, to plant, to animal to the human kingdom. This process is automatic and is controlled by the autonomic nervous system. At this juncture, however, mankind must become consciously engaged in the process of the next phase of his own evolution. At this point, the physical nature of man, using his own volition, must choose to walk the rest of way to the mountain on which the Hermit stands. The knowledge of himself and of the One Life must become "body or corporeal" knowledge, which must become established in the cells as "knowingness."[33]

The thirtieth path is called The Sun and is the planetary influence of the Sun. It is nineteen in the series of the twenty-two secret paths and connects Splendor with Foundation on the Tree of Life. The Sun is in its full expression showing all of its masculine and feminine rays, the divine masculine and the divine feminine. The boy and the girl are the same size and height indicating that self-conscious is not superior to subconscious, but are in perfect balance. It shows the modes of consciousness working in harmony to enjoy the childlike nature this stage of evolution brings. The Sun reflects a coming of age or spiritual maturity and symbolizes a candidate for membership in the fifth kingdom called Homo Spiritualis or the God/Man. On a planetary level, the Earth is also becoming a holy planet because we are inextricable linked and we share this journey together.[34]

The thirty-first path is called Judgment and is assigned the number twenty. This path is ruled by the third of the outer planets most recently discovered, called Pluto. Ancient wisdom always knew that this force existed since it has influenced the path of evolution on Earth since the beginning. The path of judgment connects Splendor to the Kingdom. The Archangel Gabriel is the influence that rules on this cardinal point of Water in the direction West. He sounds his trumpet to awaken those who are asleep in consciousness. It is on this line of force that the traveler comes into a state in the evolution of his consciousness that he and the father are one, and forever more, he will not taste "death". This is what is referred to in the bible as the "conquering of the last enemy". The cycles of death and rebirth, end. Consciousness is continuous and the traveler will no longer fall into the sleep of death. At this level, we are able to judge more justly because we now embody the law. There is no more separation. Man has now moved from the human kingdom of Homo Sapiens to that of the fifth kingdom of Homo Spiritualis.[35]

The thirty-second and last path on the Tree of Life is called The World and is assigned the number twenty-one, completing the twenty-two secret paths of wisdom. It connects Foundation to the Kingdom and is the mode of consciousness called Administrative Intelligence or cosmic consciousness. The traveler has gained dominion over all things because he has brought all elements of his own nature under the control of his higher nature; all of the so-called opposing forces are in perfect balance within him and He is at peace. He is totally free from the illusion of separation and is now qualified to work on behalf of all kingdoms below him.[36] Yeshua-Ben-Joseph was that elder brother of the human race who completed the journey and represents the light for all those coming behind up the mountain path.

The knowledge of our selves and our adventure would not be complete without an understanding of the reverse Tree. It represents the reverse side and dual aspect of man's nature. The desire for change and for the expansion of knowledge brought the prodigal son into the depth of Malkuth, in the sphere of matter, to experience the full activities of the four elements in the dimension of force and form. There is only one Tree but like a coin, it has two sides. This substantiates the experience of the duality mankind is here to reconcile. The reverse spheres are called the Qliphoth. Each reverse sphere is called a Qliphah while its obverse sphere is called a Sephirah. This mirrored tree represents the unbalanced forces we call evil. Humanity must equilibrate these forces through thought in the process of his conscious evolution. By so doing, he will bring the forces of the Qliphoth and the Sephiroth into balance within himself and the Planet. This process is accomplished by conscious understanding of the relationship of these two forces to each other. Evil cannot be destroyed but can only be understood, absorbed, harmonized and transmuted through thought. It is through this process within consciousness can he regain Unity. Only then will Malkuth truly reflect Kether.[37]

The thirty-third path is the completed and Lighted Tree of Life; it represents the Adam Qadmon or God/Man who has attained Adeptship. He is a Master Builder who has succeeded in building the temple not made with hands. This cannot be gained through membership in an organization or by being part of a certain lineage. All who enter must have walked through the "straight and narrow" gate.

The Tree of Life is a symbol of the Grand Man. It is correspondingly the symbol for the Grid of the planet Earth and the Grid of the solar system in which we live. The centers of power and consciousness in our organism also exist correspondingly at different power centers on the grid of our planet. Those planetary centers in our solar system are connected and correspond to the centers in our sphere of being. We are in an inter-related, interconnected web of life on this planet and beyond. Our destinies are bound together, forever.

As a constant reminder of this destiny, mankind was given the Masonic story and ritual that began at the beginning of time. The traveler will remove the veils. He will open the book of his own life and journey to see what he finds. The path of return must now be trodden and it is the right interpretation of his involutionary path that will accelerate his return journey on a higher arc, that of the Soul.

Table 2: Tree of Life Paths in Review

Number	Stream of Energy	Path	Force/Connects
	Spheres		**Force**
1	Crown/Kether	1	*Cosmic*
2	Wisdom/Chokmah	2	*Cosmic*
3	Understanding/Binah	3	*Cosmic*
4	Mercy/Chesed	4	*Cosmic*
5	Strength/Geburah	5	*Cosmic*
6	Beauty/Tiphareth	6	*Cosmic*
7	Victory/Netzach	7	*Cosmic*
8	Splendor/Hod	8	*Cosmic*
9	Foundation/Yesod	9	*Cosmic*
10	Kingdom/Malkuth	10	*Cosmic*
	Tarot Keys		**Connects**
0	The Fool/Aleph	11	**connects**-Crown to Wisdom
1	The Magician/Beth	12	Crown to Understanding
2	The High Priestess/Gimel	13	Crown to Beauty
3	The Empress/Daleth	14	Understanding to Wisdom
4	The Emperor/Heh	15	Wisdom to Beauty
5	The Hierophant/Vav	16	Wisdom to Mercy
6	The Lovers/Zain	17	Understanding to Beauty
7	The Chariot/Cheth	18	Understanding to Severity
8	Strength/Teth	19	Severity to Mercy
9	The Hermit/Yod	20	Mercy to Beauty

10	The Wheel of Fortune/ Kaph	21	Mercy to Victory
11	Justice/Lamed	22	Severity to Beauty
12	The Hanged Man/Men	23	Severity to Splendor
13	Death/Nun	24	Beauty to Victory
14	Temperance/Samekh	25	Beauty to Foundation
15	The Devil/Ayin	26	Beauty to Splendor
16	The Tower/Peh	27	Splendor to Victory
17	The Star/Tzaddi	28	Victory to Foundation
18	The Moon/Qoph	29	Victory to Kingdom
19	The Sun/Resh	30	Splendor to Foundation
20	Judgement/Shin	31	Splendor to Kingdom
21	The World/Tau	32	Foundation to Kingdom

Chapter Three

The Jewish Problem, Masonry and the Destiny of Man

The All-Seeing Eye: When the Eye is single, the body is filled with light

The word Masonry conjures up thoughts of secrecy, elitism, nepotism and separateness. Many believe that Masons are responsible for most of the oppression the majority of the world's population is experiencing; and this stranglehold is endemic to every country in the world. Their reach is perceived to be very wide and very deep and very deadly with control accomplished through an alliance with Lucifer. Our examination of the Tree of Life unveiled the interconnection of all aspects of Life and the web of existence we share. In this chapter, we will examine what Ancient Wisdom and the secret doctrines of occultism reveal about the truth of Masonry. How does the social fraternal organization measure up to the true meaning of Masonry?

In order to solve the issues of humanity's collective dilemma, we must take a look at what might be its core reason. Since the issue of Initiation will greatly color our curriculum for the next 2,500 years, the story of our past as a people must be looked into more deeply. The Tibetan Master known as Djwahl Khul gives us an insight into the causes, which pre-date our current memory and experience. This information he provides, sets the stage for a deeper look into the history of this ancient and powerful tradition called Masonry, its relationship with the Jewish people and how they are intertwined with humanity's destiny. This is the story of mankind's collective history on this long journey into form and his liberation out of it.

All secret orders are similar to the Masonic tradition or legend and tell us, essentially, the same thing - the story of man's descent into matter and his redemption. In every story there is a central figure, whether it be Mohammed of Islam, Jesus of Christianity, Buddha of the Hindu or Hiram Abiff of the Masonic Legend. "Jew" is a symbolic term used to describe a type of consciousness as is the term Israel.

So much has been said about this group of souls that it seems that an investigation into the arcane knowledge of this group is warranted. There is always a divine and expanded reason for all the circumstances of our lives on personal, national and global levels. The knowledge revealed by this treatise seems to bear this out and shed some light on humanity's common dilemma. This problem, so-called, has existed for many centuries and has been a great concern to the adepts and initiates who make up the Spiritual Hierarchy of our planet. It is not confined to the group we usually refer to as the Jews because the term is a symbolic term referring to almost all the peoples of the earth. They are a part of the larger human population called Israelites. The resolution of this ancient problem is essential to restoration of the harmony and understanding the world seeks. Through the struggles of this group of souls we are allowed to see the exoteric demonstrations of some of the fundamental issues that all mankind is here to work out. Djwahl Khul tells us that the problems of the Jewish people are exactly the problems of all humanity and that this ancient problem began way back in the very "night" of time when the Sun was in the constellation of Gemini, symbolic of the twin. This was before humanity emerged out of the fog of unconsciousness. It was at this time that the two pillars were set up, and as any Mason knows, these are significant landmarks in the Masonic story. This information is said to be more ancient than man and exists in the akashic records of the earth.

The astrological make-up of the Jewish people is Capricorn, which is associated with business and finance and is the sign under which the disciple takes Initiation. Their personality or form ray is the first and this first ray influence gives them the orientation toward being the "lawgiver" and makes them natural law makers. Their rising sign of Virgo connects them with the idea of the Virgin birth and of the coming of the Messiah. There is also the tendency to "pull strings" to achieve their desired objectives. We only have to look within our own nature to see all these tendencies.

The Tibetan Master makes analogies to the Jewish people, with those who have rebelled and, therefore, shows us the repeated symbolic relationship, which can be made to Cain, Lucifer, Buddha, and the Prodigal Son. They all decided to embark on a path contrary to the rest of the group. It is this same reason, which brought the Earth, known as the lost Pleiad, a non-sacred planet, on an adventure to the outer reaches of the solar system and in opposition to the sacred planets. This is what is perceived in human consciousness as the Fall. This assumption of independence is a quality expressed within the radius of power and life with the fourth or human kingdom. This act and spirit of "breaking away" clearly characterizes this group of souls. This independent nature in every man makes clear his association with and part of the Jewish family. The influence of Mercury, which rules the mind, functions very prominently in their sign and becomes the tool needed to mentally reconcile these premises of opposition in their nature. Only through use of the mind can relationships and associations be discerned.

In the latter part of the Lemurian civilization, we are told that a group of highly mentally developed souls, which also included some disciples, objected to the ideas and philosophy of the planetary Hierarchy. They, therefore, broke away from the "law of the Initiates." This took place at the time of the material development of the human consciousness - a time when the physical, emotional and mental structures of the personality were being conditioned and controlled in the human vehicle. This group of souls were those who were the early founders of the present Jewish race.[1]

The command to all disciples and initiates was to detach from all materiality. Be mindful, they were told, of the inner tendency to hold and get. As is the case with all who would seek to enter upon the path of Initiation, the mental hold of the material plane must increasingly loosen its grip on the disciple. They were repeatedly reminded that in order to enter through the gates of peace and enter into the light, they must leave behind the world of men.

As the legend continues, some of these sons of God, who were waiting outside the gates of Initiation, stood ready and waiting for the command to enter. However, the gifts they brought were all material in nature and were not what had been required of them to bring. This they presented as an act of love. Here we see an allusion to the exactness of the Masonic ritual, the alchemical process and the requirements every candidate must fulfill.

Again, the command went out to leave all behind and enter through the gates with nothing of earth. After some discussions, those who had prepared their hearts and minds rightly, entered through the portals into the light of higher consciousness. They entered free and unburdened by the weight of material possessions.

Those, on the contrary, who could not contemplate leaving behind all of the riches and gold they had, for a thousand cycles accumulated, did not proceed toward the gates. To their way of thinking they had labored long and hard for all that they had acquired. In their love for their God they were only offering, in full measure, what they had. Discipline, however, was lacking and they could not understand why their gifts would not be accepted. For the third time, the command went out to this rebellious lot to drop all they had on the ground and enter free. Three disciples revolted from the stern command while the rest obeyed. The others entered through the gates of peace and light and the three were left behind holding firmly to their treasures. In this ancient knowledge, older than any written scriptures of the world, is to be found the secret Masonic story and the slaying of the Master, by the three most closely associated with him in his death and burial.[2] These three were the founders of the modern Jewish race. These were the three advanced disciples who resented the discipline, order and exactness that true initiation demands. It requires one to reverse direction by shifting his focus away from the material and back to the essence or spirit of the matter.

With that decision to hold fast to their gold, the three disciples turned their faces toward the gates of earth.

The Masters of the Spiritual hierarchy went into private assembly to decide what would be the fate of these three disciples who loved their possessions more than they loved to serve the light. As the three stood with their faces turned toward earth a final word went out to them, this time making clear: "Hold what you have and gather more, but know no peace. Garner the fruits of mind and seek your power in wide possessions, but have no sure and certain knowledge of success or power to hold your gains".[3] These three would continue to gather and amass with no time to ever enjoy what they would accumulate.

The consequence of this decision was that, only dimly, would these three ever know of the God who watches over us all. Their knowledge would be forever veiled until the time, in the long and distant future, when the opportunity would again be presented to them. All, at this time, would stand before the gates of Light, but with empty hands. They would enter free and be accepted by the Hierarchy of masters and forever know peace.

This ancient legend tells us that the three went forth in sorrow, burdened down with treasures. This story is none other than that of the wandering Jew. Out of this group of humanity we call the Jewish people, emerged Jesus of Nazareth who was himself a Jew. He embodied in himself the way and the achievement of the Jewish people who is Humanity itself. As the representative of humanity, he was born into matter and on all points tempted, tested and triumphed. He demonstrated the ability to encounter all the circumstances of human life and to overcome. He reversed all of the earlier conditions that the three disciples were confronted with by possessing nothing. He was the first of Humanity to achieve the final initiation on the path of occultism. Previous to Him was Buddah who achieved enlightenment on the mystical path.

'The Jew embodies in himself the world Prodigal Son who is the symbol of the disciple who has not yet learned the lesson of a just sense of values.'[4] Ironically, he has been the victim of the law of light because of his inability to comply with that Law. He knows the law like no other yet consistently violates it. He does so willfully and in full knowledge of what he is doing, knowing what the results will be. By so doing he eternally becomes a victim of the Law. He has interpreted and proclaimed the law from a negative angle and this can be seen in how the Law of Moses rules most of the world yet fails to bring true legality and justice to humanity.

Those disciples who had passed on through the gates of initiation and moved forward came back into incarnation with a dim recollection of the events that separated them from their other three co-disciples. On their return to life on earth, they spoke of this happening. This might not have been the wisest thing to do because this disclosure generated feelings of antagonism, which have continued until the present. Although those disciples eventually achieved final Initiation, their disloyalty to the secret tenets of initiation still lingered. These three were also the founders of the Masonic tradition. The history of humanity, the Jewish people and Masonry is essentially the same story and is what is acted out in the Masonic ritual.

An interesting twist to this seems to be that because the three offered their material gifts in sincerity, thinking that they knew what was best, they are allowed to enact the story each year on the day when they might have entered into Light. It is these three symbolic disciples of both the Jewish peoples and the Masonic story who began the great tradition of the ancient mysteries. They know how close they came to entering into light and triumphing over death. These three vowed to stand together forever and this decision has caused a separation with the respective groups and communities they embody.

This separation extends to the body of humanity at large and this is the cause of much racial antagonism because those who had progressed now also live within this group of three.

The wandering of the Jew has allowed him to make great contributions to the world. Great men and women have been given to humanity out of this group. In spite of all these great contributions, they have been persecuted, betrayed and hounded.

The tendency of humanity to grasp and hold, and for all racial groups to preserve their racial and national identities can be seen as an outstanding characteristic of the Jewish people. There is no nation of the world that does not have its roots in this ancient race, which emerged in old Lemuria. Most of the peoples of the world stood on the path of discipleship back then. Almost all racial strains in the western world are said to be offshoots of the oldest group. The three original disciples and their family groups were the ancestors of three major racial groups and are:

1. "The Semetic race or races of biblical and modern times. The Arabs, the Afghans, the Moors, and the offshoots and affiliations of these peoples including the Egyptians. They are all descended from the eldest of the three disciples.

2. The Latin peoples and their various branches throughout the world and also the Celtic races wherever found. These are descended from the second of the three disciples.

3. The Teutons, the Scandinavians, and the Anglo-Saxons who are the descendants of the third of the three disciples."[5]

One of the major functions of the Piscean Age that just ended was to prepare new conscious bodies through higher education and emotional development. The influence of Mercury was essential in this achievement. Through education, a better understanding of

74

humanity's inter and intra-relationships with each other is becoming clearer. This, Mercury or Hermes, messenger of the Gods, is bringing to the minds of man, the knowledge of the Oneness of all the peoples of the Earth. Now that mankind is awakening to the fact of our common ancestry, we are gradually seeing the hatred and stereotypes of the Jewish people die out. The experience, which began on old Lemuria continued in the vibrations of Atlantis. On Atlantis mankind became totally immersed into matter to fully comprehend the knowledge of what the illusion of matter offers. The countries of the Middle East, Europe and the United States of America have been the primary repositories for the continuation of the idea of achieving Initiation begun on old Lemuria. The two pillars spoken of earlier in reference to the twin and the sign of Gemini is always the symbol for the gateway through which Initiation must be achieved. We see repeatedly in both the Jewish and Masonic stories the allusions to the pairs of opposites and dualism. The hint is that the goal of Initiation is to reconcile these opposites through synthesis, using the mind. As always, the soul creates scenarios in the life of the individual and humanity at large, to help him better understand the concepts to be grasped. The story of Jacob the over-comer is one such example. It shows that one must wrestle to find illumination but a way has always been made possible to achieve the goal of final liberation.

A further search into the origin and history of the peoples of our planet who are collectively called the "Israelites", lead me to Herbert W. Armstrong's book, United States and Britain in Prophecy, in which he makes an interesting case for the identification of the children of Israel. He defines Israel as consisting of twelve tribes analogous to the twelve signs of the zodiac beginning with Gad and ending with Reuben. The priestly tribe of Levi is the thirteenth and is scattered throughout the other twelve tribes. The twelve tribes are divided into three distinct groups each given a specific charge and having a specific destiny. He explains that the ten "lost" tribes of Israel also called the "House of Israel" are divided equally between the tribes Ephraim and Manessah, sons of Joseph, the youngest son of Jacob.[6]

Those familiar with the bible story of Jacob's dream in which he wrestled with the angel until daybreak will remember that due to Jacob's determination and unquenching desire for liberation, he refused to give up until the angel blessed him. This quality of spirit earned him the right to have his name changed to "Israel," which means "overcomer". Armstrong further explains this story from the book of Genesis, which illustrates how the nation of Israel was born. Joseph the eleventh and youngest son of Jacob, was sold into slavery, in Egypt by his brothers. Joseph later married an Egyptian woman who bore him two sons. The first was Ephraim and the younger Manasseh. Jacob, now blind and in the winter of his life, adopted these two lads and in a ritual, he bestowed on them a blessing. With his hands crossed, his right hand was placed on the head of Ephraim and his left hand on the head of Manessah, and he declared: "let my name be named on them."[7] He blessed Joseph and in the name of Abraham, Isaac, God and the Angel with whom he had wrestled, he pronounced that these two would grow into a multitude in the midst of the Earth. These two sons were now imbued with the title and rights of "Israel" and the divine birthright given to Israel, the overcomer.

According to Armstrong's scriptural analysis the racial and national names used by both their descendants was Israel. Due to divine intervention, the birthright - which is usually conferred upon the elder son - was given to the younger son, Manessah, because he was decreed to become the greater of the two brothers. Out of the elder brother Ephiram "a company and a multitude of nations" would come and out of this elder brother would also "spring" or would arise a "seed." The younger brother Manasseh would become a "great nation". The children of Israel would encircle the globe and number into the billions. To them was also given the birthright of "multitudinous population, material and national prosperity and dominance over other nations."[8] Armstrong has identified these two nations as Great Britain and the United States of America. Djwahl Khul, through Alice A. Bailey in The Destiny of the Nations, speaks of the great roles for which Great Britain and the United States were brought into existence and attributes the zodiacal sign of Taurus to Great Britain and Aquarius to the United States.[9] Qabalah confirms these attributions by assigning Ephraim to the sign of Taurus and Aquarius to the Manessah.

Armstrong explores the role of Judah assigned astrologically to Leo which represents the star system, Sirius, from which descends Masonry. This designation separates out the Jews as a group or remnant within the twelve tribes of Israel, called the "people of Israel." To this group of humanity, scattered in all the world, and of every race, was given the promise of carrying the scepter of spiritual power and rulership. From this group, follows a clear, unbroken leadership from Sirius to King David. This symbol of power and rulership would never pass, thus fulfilling the prophecy, "The scepter shall not pass from Judah, nor the lawgiver from between his feet, until Shiloh come; and unto him shall the gathering of the people be" (Genesis, 49:10, KJV). This promise was made to David even after the transgression of Solomon. Hidden in the mysteries of the Masonic knowledge is the fact that the scepter would pass to the feminine in the Aquarian Age. The position of equal power and rulership naturally belongs to her, she who is the creative principle behind all things in manifestation. The continuous succession to the throne of David from Palestine takes us across geographic and spiritual time to the reigning monarchy of Great Britian.[10] The deep Masonic history of Great Britain had its beginnings across time and place from Sirius into the Middle East, with Egypt being the great repository of the mysteries. The sphinx has the face of a man, which is the symbol of the Aquarian and the present Age. The body of a lion is a reference to the sign of Leo, the polar opposite sign of Aquarius. Together with the pyramid of Giza, an Initiation chamber, these symbols point to the goal of this Age, the achievement of man's full sovereignty and consciousness. In this Age the masculine and feminine will be united in the conscious manifestation of the true Masonic story. This forms the bedrock of the intellectual and spiritual destiny given to mankind. The reigning monarch has emerged as the exoteric holder of the royal and priestly symbol of the true position to which the feminine in every race, culture and station was born. She holds this position of relative power for the Feminine Elder of the Temple, the High Priestess to emerge. She is the Intelligence of Unity who accomplishes the splendor of Oneness symbolized by the All-seeing Eye of Masonry. Her shared governance with the masculine will see true brotherhood and inclusiveness established on Earth. The Feminine Principle who created the rule of law will see to its administration. It was to Great Britain the charge given to teach the world "the rule of law" and to nurture the United States of America, the child of Aquarius, into fulfilling its role in the destiny of humanity in this Age. As stated in *The Celestine Prophecy*, by James Redfield, the child is to become a refined version of the parent.

The lost tribes of Israel were to remain hidden until the "end times" when the Christ will return, and Masters of Wisdom will govern the Earth who are the true Master Masons.[11] We are now in the throws of an explosion of consciousness the world has not yet seen. The true spiritual destiny for which mankind has been made ready through all the succeeding forms of government is now being established on Earth. The struggle, which began on Atlantis between Matter and Spirit, the feminine and the masculine, rich and poor, intellect and instinct will finally come to an end and all humanity will realize the vision of liberation from separation and ignorance.

The story of Masonry is the story of mankind for which Jews and Gentiles, Black and White, Dark and Light and all the other pairs of opposites are but symbols. To understand the drama we have chosen to play out on this earth stage, we must examine closely the meaning of the two pillars of Solomon's Temple, one black and the other white. They represent the pairs of opposites that underpin all of our conflicts, pain and feelings of separation. The understanding of the principles they symbolize and a grasp of their inner meaning hold the key to the solution of the human dilemma on all levels of human existence.

In our examination of the Tree of Life, Binah, the principle of Divine Feminine, represents the Black pillar, and Chokmah, the principle of Divine Masculine, represents the White pillar and the dual aspects of the One Self. We will examine the nature and origin of these apparently separate forces because they represent the essences of Water and Fire respectively, the essential elements for the formation and sustenance of all life. On careful examination of the alchemical water, we find that it is the same as cosmic fire symbolized by the blood. Scientists will discover that in the blood are the elements that connect all humans to a single origin.

Mankind, among whom are the masters of wisdom from the planet Sirius, brought the blueprint of our origin and purpose to this planet to play out our different roles, that of villains and saints. When we can remember that we have taken turns playing those roles, we will have more compassion and less judgment of each other.

In the scroll held in the lap of the high priestess are the records of all that we have done and the divine laws governing these activities.

She is a symbol of memory and feelings and represents the thirteenth path on the Tree of Life, the number of transformation and change. We can only change when we can remember. Earth is known as a water planet with its occult relationship with fire intertwined to produce life. To understand matter, man must study the nature of alchemical fire and alchemical water and their relationship to each other in the medium of air.

We are told by the Masters of wisdom that the temple of Solomon is an architectural symbol of the Great Work played out in the building of the Temple not made with hands. If we have all been commissioned to be builders, it must be concluded that we are all Masons. We all must return to the state of consciousness we once held before embarking on this long journey into night. We are further told that what makes us a Mason is obligation. This obligation requires that each of us will return home and need appropriate vehicles to take us home. We are obliged to begin to collect the materials needed to build that house or temple in Jerusalem, that home of light where spirit can always dwell with us.

In every generation and in every cycle of expression, a certain group of souls who represent the older members of the human race, men and women who have attained a certain level of spiritual development, are entrusted with being the keepers of the ancient or occult teachings. What is sometimes missing from the perspective of the public is that the consciousness exhibited by the exoteric order of masonry does not constitute all of what masonry is about. What seems separative in expression by many Masons is reflective and representative of what is in need of healing in the consciousness of Mankind in general. What is not seen, however, are the groups of souls of every race and culture who comprise the inner Lodge. These individuals are not readily identified as the Master Masons they are, by their social or material standing in society. The members of the outer Lodge do not know most of them and would probably not associate with them. They work tirelessly to establish the Divine Plan on Earth by keeping the vision clear for making a living temple of this planet. They influence the outer Lodge to build the institutions of learning, which provide the framework for mental and emotional development of mankind throughout all fields of education.

The Aquarian Age marks the returning point in the evolutionary path. This is the time when the ancient or occult teachings will be made plain. The secrets of the "secret orders" will increasingly be revealed. The truth, in part, for that concealment was more a function of mankind's maturity and capacity to receive truth. No information was really being kept from the public. All the secrets spoken about are in plain view for everyone to see. To be able to read these secrets, however, requires one to be able to see beyond appearances. Individuals who are emotionally and mentally too immature to perceive truth cannot grasp advanced concepts. College degrees do not necessarily equip an individual either; it is the soul that must be ripe and not be materially minded.

The goal of the Piscean Age was to provide the educational preparation necessary to build stronger mental and emotional bodies capable of grasping and holding the new inflow of consciousness coming into the body of mankind from above and beyond. The age of Pisces was also the age of idealism, devotion and paternalism. Over the last twenty-one hundred years, we created idols of individuals who we deemed to be greater than ourselves only to be disappointed at the only possible outcome. This apparent failure was designed to goad us on to turn inside ourselves to discover the greatness we possess. Jesus, the elder brother and leader of the Piscean Age, told us "you and I are one", "we are joint heirs together," but mankind turned a deaf ear to the idea that He was not their god but their brother. The responsibility for ownership of this great ancestry, heritage and power seem too unbelievable for humanity.

Mankind is being challenged to go within and to realize his sovereignty and power and he must do so if he is to return home. The emotional experiences of the last Age on this water planet took mankind to the depth of his emotional adventure. He came to have this baptismal experience because it is through these deep and profound emotional experiences he would come to know himself and by so doing, know God. It is water that contains the secrets of our past and the road map to our future. In the depth of water are the fires of mind, where the mental and emotional bodies are expanded.

The story of Masonry is the allegorical story of the master builder, Hiram Abiff, and his assignment to build the Temple of Solomon under instructions from Solomon's father, David. David, the man of war and duality could not construct the temple, which requires a consciousness of oneness to build. The task was left to his son Solomon who had evolved that consciousness. During the building of the temple, Hiram was confronted and slain by the threefold powers of the "cosmic night", known as the three ruffians symbolic of perverted thought, uncurbed emotions and destructive actions.[12] Through the three degrees or initiations in the Blue Lodge, the aspirant ends his long journey and finds liberation as a Master Mason in the third degree.

The journey of every individual into mortal existence is symbolized by admission into the Masonic Order. The Masonic story tells us that man came into existence from the mystical "East", the source of spiritual knowledge. Our experience here is spent in the symbolic "West", the place of darkness that is the opposite pole of our origination. Every candidate for admittance enters in the West of the Lodge. He is brought there through the process of birth as a babe into a state of unconsciousness, having forgotten much in his descent into form. When the candidate, the Entered Apprentice, is asked from whence he came, his response is "from the West". In his state of darkness or ignorance, he perceives that he originated in the West.

The admission into the Lodge is also indicative of the individual's entry into this Earth Lodge and that he existed somewhere, in another world, prior to coming into this Lodge. He came into form to establish his relationship with the physical. When he leaves this human sojourn and has completed this segment of his soul career, he will move on out of this Earth Lodge to another world befitting of his level of mastery.[13]

The Masonic apron, with which each Mason is invested, is worn over the reproductive area of the body and is symbolic of man's entry into physical form through the reproductive process. The apron is made of lamb's skin, which symbolizes his innocence, and is an allusion to the sign of Aries, the first sign of the zodiac. The design of the apron is that of a triangular flap, the symbol of the soul, sitting on a square, which represents the body that forms the personality vehicle. This illustrates the relationship of the soul to the physical body. A soul infused personality is the goal and obligation of every Mason or individual on Earth. This is also termed the completion of the "Great Work."[14]

The five-pointed and five-sided figure the apron forms symbolizes man, and the five senses with which we experience. The candidates are encouraged to regard their aprons, their body of flesh and covering for the soul, as the most precious gift they could be given. The three-sided triangular flap and the four-sided square also symbolize the seven-fold nature of man and represent the "perfect Lodge."[15]

The number seven directly relates to the seven liberal arts and sciences. No one can evolve to true mastery without concrete knowledge and the ability to reason rationally and objectively. He must be able to reason on all subjects eloquently. He grows gradually and in stages as he progresses through the physical, emotional, mental and spiritual planes of life towards the experience of true liberation; his interpretation of the subjects learned must also be in accordance with divine law. Labor and service are fundamental to growth because they provide for the development of the sense centers that later become the channels for the expression of spiritual truths.[16]

Each of us, at birth, has been given three lesser lights. First, are the "suns" which represents our higher spiritual aspirations. Second is the Moon, which reflects the aspirations of the "Sun" in our daily lives, and represents the application of the intellect or our reasoning ability. Third, is the "Master of the Lodge" or "will power", which allows us to master our own lives by keeping the energies of the lower nature under the control of the "Higher Mind." The Master striking his gavel to indicate his control over the Lodge, demonstrates this fact, and in obedient response, the brethren come to order.[17]

This assistance given to man allows him to understand the form of his "Lodge", his own nature and how it is constituted. By these lesser lights, he is able to comprehend the geometry of his composition— the length, breadth, height and depth of his own being. Man also comes to know that his body and his soul are the "holy ground" on which the altar of his own spiritual life should be built. On this altar, no defiling or debasing habits are to be placed.[18] By these Lights, Man is able to perceive how Strength, Wisdom and Beauty, the three supporting pillars of his Lodge, were used in the construction of his own Lodge. In the final analysis, he is able to understand that there is a mystical ladder with many steps that he must travel upward to the encircling Light of Love in which we all live, move and have our being.

Receiving the apron is a symbol of Man's birth into the world and with this, the foundation stone of his spiritual life is laid and implanted in him. With his obligation to develop and erect a superstructure upon that foundation, he is placed in the northeast corner of the lodge. Two paths represented by the pillars of light and dark are opened to the candidate, and the northeast corner is the dividing place between the two.[19]

The direction north is a symbol of man's unenlightened state, the unknown and his greatest fears. It is that place in him where the light is latent and has not yet risen above the materialism and sensuality of his lower nature. What is intended for him to see is that on the other side of him is the path that leads to the perpetual Light in the East.

As is the case of every human, he is always put in a position to go forward toward the Light or to return into darkness. This ceremony, therefore, is the comprehensive enactment of the first degree, which portrays the entrance of all men into physical life and then, into spiritual life. This degree or initiation is one of preparation, self-discipline and purification. It is analogous to the sacrament of baptism, which takes place at the font in the entrance to the church, and for the aspirant at the beginning of his spiritual career.[20] In the ancient mystery schools, long periods of preparation were required of all aspirants in the achievement of mental and emotional discipline and balance before they were allowed to proceed to the next initiation upon the path of self-knowledge. This stage in his self-unfolding will reveal to him the secrets of his mental nature and the principles underlying life on this plane of existence.

The initiation called the Fellow Craft degree is the next stage upon the journey. Through the Fellow Craft degree, the second ruffian symbolized by uncurbed emotions, is brought under the control of the mind through the application of the knowledge gained in the study of the seven liberal arts and sciences. Before he can progress further on the path, he must demonstrate his ability to master his emotions, to be poised under difficult conditions, and to show kindness in the face of unkindness. He has arrived at the knowledge that all personal manifestations are governed by impersonal principles and he has transmuted personal affections into impersonal compassion. With the aid of the understanding he has gained thus far, the aspirant becomes aware of the "sacred symbol" present in the center of the Lodge and his own being, which is the divine spark of God innate within all life. The ability to find that sacred symbol requires that he apply the exactness of thought, word and action as symbolized by the principles of the *plum-rule*, the *square* and the *level* used in the building trade. He must be ready to walk the way of the cross. He must work the rough ashlar of his own nature into the perfect cube of which his own life is a type.[21]

The triangular flap of the apron in this degree is turned down upon the rectangular portion as a symbol of the permeation of the higher spiritual nature of the soul into the personality. The aspirant now becomes more conscious of the obstacles of the outer life to the path of his spiritual life. Upon careful contemplation, he realizes that the difficulties placed in his life are placed there to assist him in developing the latent and potential good in him. He begins to realize that "just as the rough ashlar can only be squared and perfected by chipping and polishing, he can only be made perfect by toil and suffering. He sees that difficulties, adversity and persecution serve a "beneficent purpose." His wages are purity of heart and mind and this is what he can expect from the Employer who sent him into this distant world to collect the materials needed to build *the temple not made with hands eternal in the heavens.*"[22]

The aspirant who has mastered this degree or initiation has passed from the north side of ignorance in the Lodge and now stands in the Southeast corner on the meridian of moral illumination. He is still limited, however, by a lack of full understanding of himself and the mysteries of his own nature.

Before he can gain fuller self-knowledge and adeptship, symbolized by the degree of Master Mason, he must pass through the greatest and final trial of death to the former Man. He must experience a rebirth or regeneration and be raised an incorruptible Man made possible by triumph over the lower nature. The symbolic elder brother of the Masonic Legend who successfully made the journey out of darkness into light, Hiram Abiff, corresponds to Jesus, of the Christian faith.

The candidate for this degree is appropriately adorned with the apron and the decorations befitting one who has overcome. He is now lord of himself, able to govern the Lodge that is within himself. He has passed through the three degrees of purification and self-perfection. He has squared, leveled and harmonized his triple nature of body, soul and spirit.[23] The essence of the Masonic career then, as taught by the three degrees, is the inward journey of the natural man to the god-man. This is made possible by the true surrender of his old life and the loosing of his soul to later save it. He raises from the dead, a Master, a just man made perfect with a larger consciousness and greater faculties. He is an efficient instrument for use by the Great Architect in his plan of rebuilding the Temple of fallen humanity. He is now capable of initiating and advancing other men to participate in the same Great Work.[24]

Only he, who arrives at a place within himself where he hungers and thirsts to know himself, will venture out beyond the lure of social and charitable associations to embark on this journey. Have no doubt, for every traveler on this plane, the hour will arrive when he will come to himself and consciously decide to begin the journey "home."

The stories of the Jewish people and the Masonic legend speak of the three advanced disciples and the three ruffians, respectively. These three are symbolic of the three disciples closest to the master Jesus and to Hiram Abiff. The astrology of the Jewish nation offers us a great insight into the issues facing Mankind. They have agreed to come into incarnation as a group and as a "particularized aspect" of the whole of mankind to help us see more clearly the glories and pains of our decisions. What is of utmost importance, however, is the ability to make the correct interpretations of our experiences. How does Man know if he is making the correct interpretation? An ancient rule of thumb is to look at what is happening in his manifest world. The law or guidelines for our involution and evolution are written in our cells. Our DNA carry the blueprint of all that we will ever want to know. We are here on this experience not so much to learn, but to unfold the knowledge of who we really are. The result of correct interpretation of life experiences is "peace." When one is experiencing peace and I mean true peace, not so-called peace based on blame and escape of any kind, that peace is lasting and is only achieved when the idea of separation is changed, not just intellectually, but in all the cells.

To better understand our experience in incarnation, we will look at the information from Ageless Wisdom concerning Capricorn in the human experience here on Planet Earth. This is the story of the three associate builders of the Masonic legend and the story of the three disciples of the Jewish story who presented themselves for initiation. These groups of three are the representatives of the three major strains that comprise the racial groups of Humanity. The particular astrological construct of these three helps us identify the issues, which lie at the core of mankind's destiny. He must eventually come to understand this destiny and evolve his final liberation.

The sign Capricorn is the personality Ray of the Jewish people and, consequently, of humanity as a whole. The personality ray of an individual or place is the sign in which the Sun was present at the time of birth. It indicates the individual's ability to respond to the Soul. Additionally, it represents the level of soul matter integrated into his vehicle.[25] Capricorn is the tenth sign. As with all signs of the zodiac, it is a composite of three decanates, which in this case are three earth signs. Therefore, Taurus and Virgo complete this triplicity. Their accompanying rulers are Saturn, Venus and Mercury, respectively. A closer look at these three aspects will give us deeper insight into the disciple preparing for initiation in this sign. Capricorn is the tenth sign of the zodiac and is the sign in which the aspirant becomes an initiate on the mountain of transfiguration. It is an Earth sign ruled by the Planet Saturn, which is called our celestial teacher.

Saturn is also the planet, which conditions the point in evolution where choice becomes possible. Saturn is synonymous with Chronos, the father of time, who essentially said "I have all the time in the world, so I will take you over and over the lessons you are here to unfold and understand, until you get it!"

The unregenerated Capricorn can be cruel, hard, materialistic, proud, selfish, ambitious and egotistical. Capricorn also rules the knees and it is only when the aspirant has learned to bend his knees in humility before the Initiator that he will be allowed to pass through the gate of initiation. He must pass through this gate on his knees and not standing up demanding what he feels he deserves.[26]

The Capricorn experience is the symbolic reference to the point in the evolution of the soul where Saturn - the Lawgiver, in Capricorn, imposed the law of karma on the Jewish people or humanity after being transfigured as Moses was on Mount Sinai. The occult meaning of the word "karma" is the law of action and reaction. Therefore, humanity and the Jewish people are the clearing-house for the Law of Karma on the many cycles on the wheel of life.[27]

The Mount of Transfiguration represents the planet Venus where love and mind meet in the state of Christ consciousness. The transfiguration took place before "all men", an allusion to all the cells in the body being present and transformed. The aspirant thus becomes a new person. It was on the mountain that Moses received the vision of his mission. He was instructed to "go up into Jerusalem," which is symbolically the place of death and peace represented by the sign of Pisces. Yeshua Ben Joseph or Jesus was to carry forward the promise of salvation as the reincarnation of Moses, fulfilling the law given by Saturn.[28]

It is the planet Saturn that prepares the soul for release from form. Saturn provides the limiting, restricting influences in the life of the aspirant that allows him to see his choices more clearly. It is here that the individual is able to make the decisions and apply the discrimination needed to make the necessary changes. Saturn destroys whatever prevents the free expression of the soul by providing the ideal conditions, situations and right opportunity for the aspirant to achieve initiation.

Under the influence of Venus and the ruler of the next decanate, Taurus, the aspirant moves from the state of desire for matter to aspiration for Spirit. Taurus, the sign of the Bull, is very closely associated with money or gold in our society and was seen as a worthwhile token of love. However, the lack of understanding of the need to transmute the concrete into the abstract caused the offering to be rejected. This journey in the sign of Gemini, which began back in the distant past of mankind's history led humanity on the path to discovering the true nature of the two aspects of his nature. The Bull of Form (gold or matter) must eventually clash with the Bull of Life (Spirit) and in that meeting an illuminating consciousness will be born. It is Venus who confers illumination on the aspirant through the application of pure reason. Through reason, the aspirant receives the revelation of the universality of life. Venus establishes in the disciple the relationship of man-to-man, and nation-to-nation and is the link that connects the heart with the mind because the "eye of illumination" or "the eye of the bull" is now opened.[29]

In the third decanate Virgo— ruled by Mercury, the aspirant in Capricorn develops greater illumination of the mind. Mercury, also known in Greek mythology as Hermes - the Master of illusion, is the Divine Messenger. It is in Virgo, the sign of the Virgin Mother and the Christ child that Mercury brings the aspirant out of the womb of time and matter into the light of the infant Christ. It is in the Virgo region of the body, the small intestines, that matter is transformed into chyle or "liquid gold" in the blood. From this cave in the rocky mountain of Capricorn, gold is mined and the aspirant is transformed and begins to sense the first stirring of the Christ within. He, the Mountain goat, then makes his steady climb up the mountain of attainment to final liberation in Capricorn. Mercury makes clear the relationship of old to new, of the past to the present and of the past to the future so the aspirant is able to see the illusion of matter.

The sign of Capricorn, through its three decanates, provides humanity with Opportunity, Illumination and Brotherhood. These are the gifts that the Father/Mother desires to confer upon humanity in the Age of Aquarius, if he will prepare himself to receive them.

The rising sign of the Jewish nation is Virgo. The rising sign is the soul aspect of the individual and is that influence which gives purpose

91

to the soul and holds the secret for the future of the individual in incarnation. Virgo symbolizes the subordination of matter to spirit in the person of the Christ. The Virgo or Virgin Mother influences the soul's destiny. It nurtures and protects the "Christ-child" for birth in Capricorn.

The first Ray of Will and Power is the nature of the vibration expressed by the soul of the Jewish nation and is also called the "destroyer ray." The first ray is associated with law, politics and government. The Divine Will emanating from Shamballah impulses humanity and all life, through this Ray. This energy is responsible for bringing the aspirant to initiation and gives the feeling of not wanting to participate with the group, but to do things independently. This first ray quality is needed to force issues and determine results but not at the expense of the group.

The great lesson of the first ray soul is comradeship that can only be achieved through the deepening love of nature. The great band of souls, the true remnants of Judah are of every race, ethnicity and nation and are the initiates who are called "Israel" or "He who is like God". They are the Master Masons, the Initiates who have made themselves ready to serve humanity on this lost Pleiad, the planet of Alcyone, the Star of Intelligence.

As we now see, we the peoples of planet Earth are the overcomers; we are all the children of Israel, one and all. We are the children of the three aspects of Deity, which cannot be separated or else we all perish together. We each carry the life-sustaining elements for the survival of the whole. The governments of our world hold within their constitutions and governing principles, the spiritual symbols of masonry. When understood and used as was intended, for the benefit of mankind, an eager and thirsty humanity will be readily fed.

To the United States, Great Britain and Russia are given the responsibilities to see that the peoples of the world are fed physically, emotionally and spiritually.[30] Their failure to carry out these responsibilities to which they were called can be of dire consequence to a desperate world. However, it is to Great Britain, and the eldest of the two brothers, that the responsibility is entrusted to ensure that the Divine Plan for the whole world is carried out. It must be carried out in fairness and wisdom with no regard for station of birth, class, money or race and under the rule of law. The true Master Mason, by virtue of his own overcoming, knows that God has no favorites but that all peoples are one. He knows first-hand the truth of the oneness of the human family and will prevail in seeing to it that no one is left behind. It is the duty and obligation of these and all nations to supervise the equitable distribution of the abundant resources the Divine Mother has made available on Earth for all her children. This I know will become a reality on our planet when the spirit, instead of the form, is lived out in all levels of our government.

To the United States of America, this great nation who is both the child and the brother of England, the baton was passed to develop and carry out the ideal of Masonry. The founding fathers that were themselves mostly Masons established Masonry in the original thirteen colonies. They had written on the seal of the country the destiny to which America was created. The seal bears the motto, Novus Ordo Seclorum, which means 'A New World Order', one based on the premise of the Declaration of Independence, which states that all men are created equal and are imbued with the inalienable right to Liberty and Justice for all. The symbol of Venus-Urania stands in New York harbor with her torch in one hand and her book or scroll in the other. It contains the history of the whole human family and all life to which she gave birth. She, who is a symbol of Liberty and Justice, is the constant reminder to all those who would lead this great nation, of the charge given to them by God. In America, the resolution of the two previous ideals of Lemuria and Atlantis, the ideas of the true relationship between spirit and matter must come together in understanding. The vision of brotherhood entrusted to America, the keeper of this vision, is a great responsibility to humanity in the Aquarian Age. The adepts and masters of wisdom from Atlantis are now here again to oversee the establishment of this New World Order; one based on love, inclusiveness and the sovereignty of each individual.[31]

New York City has been spoken of as the place of the New Jerusalem and the place where the remnants of the thirteen tribes of Israel are gathered from every corner of the globe. It is, therefore, fitting that the United Nations is located there. I am confident that the United States will continue to grow, thus making itself a more perfect vehicle for the manifestation of the divine plan for the whole world. America expresses the will-to-love and is most sensitive to the impulses from the Spiritual Hierarchy, the overseer of the New World Order that is now being anchored on the planet.

The will-to-power is given to Great Britain for the distribution of the rule of law and right justice throughout the world; this nation forms the other half of the Love-Wisdom brotherhood shared with the United States. The wisdom aspect of Great Britain gives it the ability to oversee the administration of the divine plan to the world. This it knows more than most having had its rulership in every corner of the globe due to its will-to-synthesis.

To Russia is given the will-to-be and to rule creatively because of its great emphasis on human values.[32] These three nations and all the other governmental centers of power around the globe will in this round do humanity proud. I am sure of it!

Chapter Four

The Aquarian Age - The Repairer of the Breach

Isis-Urania:Bringer of the Aquarian Age

The planet Uranus, the planet of esoteric and occult mysteries, is ushering in the Age of Aquarius. In this Age covering the next 2,100 years, we will achieve the goal of Ageless Wisdom, which is to see the feminine aspect of Deity restored to its former glory. Then the destiny of mankind will have come full circle.

In Qabalistic Tarot symbolism, the sign of Aquarius is given as Key 17 or the Star. Aquarius is co-ruled by both Uranus and Saturn.[1] Saturn is the planet of tradition and has been mankind's celestial teacher from the beginning; it provides the solid and concrete life opportunities for the evolution of man's consciousness while he is in form. The symbols associated with this Age give us much insight into the message and the focus of the One Self in the Age of Aquarius. Key "0" or the Fool is the symbol for the planet Uranus in Qabalistic Tarot.

The Fool: symbol of the planet Uranus

The planet Uranus is the influence of superconsciousness and is located above and beyond the pineal center in the body. It is the Sun in Uranus, which is affecting the next twenty-one hundred years of human evolution. Its most direct influence on human evolution is the impact it has on the seventh chakra in the body; that is the pineal gland ruled by Mercury.

The Magician: the transparent medium of divine intelligence into matter

The pineal gland symbolized by the Magician or Hermes is like an eye located in the middle of the brain with its lens turned upward to the Sun. It is through the aperture of this lens that the stream of consciousness coming from the higher realms, enter the brain.[2] These vibratory frequencies in turn, stimulate the pituitary gland which is the Master gland in the body; it controls the other endocrine glands associated with all the remaining chakras. These impulses in turn stimulate the brain and the entire nervous system to set up a new and higher rate of vibration in the whole body. This is how higher and more expansive levels of consciousness are achieved in the body.

The journey of humanity in form, since the Garden of Eden, has consisted of the struggle between the pairs of opposites such as good and bad, wrong and right, etc.

The High Priestess: Keeper of the Arcane Mysteries

The struggle between the pairs of opposites is in direct relationship with the choices presented to Eve or the physical expression of humanity in the Garden of Eden. When Eve, who represents the body, responded to the choice from a place of need, to satisfy the needs of the five senses, mankind became caught in a spiral of sense gratification. The scriptures indicate that as long as the woman obeyed the "Lord" or the superconscious aspect of Life, all went well, until "she" chose instead to obey the body or matter.

It is the urge to satisfy the senses and the needs of the flesh, which has kept mankind on the wheel of life through the twelve signs of the zodiac for eons. With the aid of Mercury, which influences the function of the pineal gland, mankind has allowed the light of superconsciousness to be reflected through the aperture in the pineal gland. A large number of humanity's consciousness is now turned in the direction of Home. This allows for the turn of the lens in the pineal, just like with a sunflower turns upward toward the sun to receive the rays of superconsciousness.

During this long period, which was dominated by human sensation, the true nature of woman in relationship to the masculine principle or the self-conscious aspect has been hidden or veiled. During this period, the Moon was said to be hiding Uranus. In Key 17, we see the image of a woman who is called Isis-Urania who is nude and is pouring water from two vases. The esoteric symbolism of nakedness is the implication that there is no shame, nothing to hide and therefore indicates that it is now time for the revelation of all secrets.

Earlier in the series we had Key Two, the High Priestess sitting between the two pillars in the temple holding a scroll, which contains the laws upon which the "secrets" of life are written. This lady Isis called the Star, is the same lady, the High Priestess, but at a different stage in the evolution of human and global consciousness. She is no longer clothed but is naked because she now reveals the secrets she has kept hidden since the beginning of time. It is fair to deduce from the symbols we are given, that in this Age there will be an uncovering and a diving into the "waters" of subconscious to find the answers to the individual and global problems that face us. One of the attributions given to Key 17 is that of revelation. We can, therefore, conclude that we will have some great revelations over this cycle of the Cosmic Year of

Aquarius. The higher self reveals itself to the mind of man through symbolic representations. In order to uncover what this Age holds for us, it is important that we train ourselves in the meaning of universal symbols. Symbols are the letters of a universal language; the alphabet or the rules of the language must be learned in order to decipher the information that is given.

As a possible clue to what might be unveiled, the symbols in the Key give us some hints. We know that water is the primary aspect of this discovery. The High Priestess is the holder of the book or scroll that holds the secrets and she is the primary symbol for water in all of the twenty-two Keys. Ageless Wisdom tells us that water is the Root Matter and the reflection of Spirit in Matter and it is associated with the Moon. This same water is described as the "Blood of the Earth" with its electro-magnetic currents coursing through the arteries.[3] Cycles, rhythms and vibrations are other meanings given to this Feminine Aspect. She is the builder of all forms through the medium of Light in the form of Sound. All forms occupy a certain wavelength on the Light spectrum and carry a certain vibration and frequency. We are told that in order to have dominion over anything, we must first define or name it. In the Emerald Tablet of Hermes, we are told that all things are from the One and all things have their birth from the One Thing by adaptation and that the Sun is our Father and the Moon our Mother. From this premise then, we will reveal to ourselves how all these things are connected to the WORD or SOUND, which entered into the VOID or the Great Deep and became Flesh or matter.

To further decipher the inner message of Key 17, and through it the Aquarian Age that is here, we will look deeper into the meaning of the Key it symbolizes. The Hebrew letter name for Key 17 is Tzaddi to which Qabalah assigns "fish-hook", which is the combination of two names already given in the Qabalistic assignations. "Fish" is the name given to Nun represented by Key 13 to which is attributed, Death or Transformation. This Key is the symbol for the sign of Scorpio and is ruled by the planet Mars. The word "hook" is the name given to Vav the Hebrew name for Key 5 called the Hierophant, which represents the sign of Taurus and is ruled by the planet Venus; the function of "hearing" or of sound is also associated with the Hierophant. The Hierophant, as we might remember, is the extension of the Emperor, which is the union of the earthly and spiritual Man. He is the symbol of what Man is to become— Spirit in flesh. To achieve this state we can see that the actions of Mars, which control the Scorpio region of the body must act upon the Venus center, the throat chakra in order to achieve the unveiling, disclosure and discovery, which is the promise of the Aquarian Age. This throat or Venus center is known as the "power" center in the body related to speech and communication. When these Taurus centers in the head are activated, the aspirant must speak with truth, love and beauty, the attributes of Venus. Out of his "mouth" must issue the healing waters of life, which at the same time constructively destroys and heals. This output of sound vibration, which issues from the illumined Man radiates out into the cosmos and by so doing is affects an alteration in the frequency of everything in the web of life.[4] The Hierophant is the Revealer and Key 17 is the symbol of that revelation. Through the influence of the Mars force the process of dissolution acts upon the centers of hearing in the brain thus enabling mankind to hear the Voice of the Inner Teacher, the Hierophant— the Voice of the Silence.

The Star seen in Key 17 is the same as that shown on the triangle or capstone of the Egyptian pyramid. It is also the Blazing Star of Masonic symbolism and stands for the quintessence of the Alchemist, which is the Master Mason of Freemasonry. This capstone is the fifth element of the pentagram and symbolizes the enlightened or regenerated Man of which the Hierophant is a symbol.[5] It is also the symbol of the First Pope, Peter. Jesus asked Peter: 'Who do you say I am?' Peter's response was: 'thou art Christ the son of the Living God.' Jesus' response to him was: flesh and blood did not reveal that knowledge to you because it was no ordinary knowing. Peter had to have developed the "inner hearing" by which the things of a higher order are revealed and thus his ability at "recognition" that Jesus was indeed the Son of God. This response established him as the "rock" upon which the "church" was built. It is this inner ability that separates the true adept from the average human being. An important characteristic of the God-man in comparison to the ordinary man is that there are no outward distinguishing marks. Only by the development of "inner sight", of which "inner hearing" is a part, can one really know the members of the fifth race. It is to this high state that all humanity is now gathering in humility at the portal of the temple seeking admittance.

The Hierophant is the symbol for the spiritual attainment for humanity. In him are all five senses spiritualized. There is no guile in him. He can hear, taste, see, smell and feel the needs of his fellow men because he KNOWS intimately their cry. He has walked the same evolutionary journey being traversed by every aspect of the One Life. The inner secrets of that Oneness has been revealed to him and he is now the representation of that which has been revealed.[6]

No one who is in separation and, who has not reasoned out the fact that all humans of all races, ethnicity, social and religious beliefs, and educational backgrounds are One, will ever know the inner secrets of life. One must know that all life is of the One and from the One but simply at different stages of unfolding that reality. Without this understanding, one cannot consider oneself to be liberated. In this regenerated man, all the pairs of opposites have been reconciled. This new man will not be a rarity in the new Age of Aquarius but will be representative of the New World Order in which spiritual unity is the established reality. Under the leadership of this new consciousness, the Brotherhood of Man and not the brotherhood of a few will be established forever.

Another hint given us as to the work to be accomplished in this Age is an analysis of the number of the Key itself, the number 17. The number seven symbolizes the Chariot, the sign of Cancer, and the personality vehicle, while the Number One represents the Higher Mind; and so, the influence of the Higher Mind operating through the personality vehicle will dominate in the Aquarian Age. The reality of preparing our vehicles for the perfect manifestation of God in form will now become an actual reality in the Aquarian Age. In summary, the personality vehicle will become the 'Intelligence of the House of Influence' for the One Will. On the two vases carried by Isis are blue ovals, which allude to Key O and to Akasha, the source from which all things came and to which all things are returning. This is more clearly suggested by the fact that with one vase she lifts the water out of the pool and with the other she returns it to the pool, the Great Ocean of universal subconsciousness out of which all things issued forth into manifested form, and to which all this must return. The number One is the symbol for Mercury and Hermes the messenger of the gods. He is the Transparent Intelligence who expresses the divine plan through the new regenerated vehicle, the personality.

To make the goals of the spiritualization of man a reality in this Age, he must remember; because the path of illumination is one of unfolding the god we already are. This can only be achieved by the combined actions of the feminine and masculine centers in the body, under supervision of the Higher Self. This Path of Return is not an event but a journey, which individually and collectively must be taken and achieved together.

All the Qabalistic representations given to us by the Keys, repeatedly point us to the masculine and feminine forces at work in the human body and that of the planet. We see the relationships and the dance of the elements of fire and water in their "sexual interactions" in all things in nature as they are always moving toward the creation of a more expansive representation of themselves.

The Root of Water is assigned to the High Priestess and one of its attributions is the Uniting Intelligence, referenced by the two pillars of black and white, she sits between. The sexual representations of the palm and the pomegranates are other clues to the role and function of the influence of the Scorpio center. Reproduction, associated with the Scorpio center, is the outcome of this influence in the concept of Unity. She is the direct link of the Christed One with the Father or source of all knowledge. Through the person of the High Priestess, in the representation of Isis, the connection with our distant home is being made in the Age of Aquarius.

When the self-conscious aspect of man is in right relation to his Higher Self then man makes decisions that are more harmonious. Man then becomes a conscious transparent vehicle for the expression of super- consciousness in form. He is able to grasp and come to grips with the problems of his daily life. It is this ability which ushers him on a higher turn of the spiral and on his way through the "gates of heaven" and back to his home of self- knowledge.

The planet Uranus is also known in Qabalah as being associated with new and original technology. It is this frequency of energy, which comes from the source and is acquainting man with what he already possesses in his memory bank or his DNA. We have been introduced, or rather more appropriately reminded of wave- form motion, the significance of which is that through the water in the pool, humanity will begin to remember the true nature of water, its many applications and his own origin.

In Key "0", the Fool symbolizes all aspects of human expression. It is in this "egg" that all life is contained. While the High Priestess is the symbol of Unity, the Fool is the symbol of and stands for what is before all beginnings and represents the gateway to heaven itself. He also represents the fact that to many, those things which are of the spirit appear as foolishness. The Fool is young in appearance and could be seen as either a lad or a lass alluding to the fact that God is both male and female and at the same time is neither. This symbol of the Fool also makes us aware of the children who are among us and are rapidly coming into our planet. These children are our future selves. We are seeing ourselves give birth to aspects of consciousness we have evolved and have longed to see manifested on earth.

The Fool represents the most perfect and complete aspects of us. Each generation coming in will represent even greater and more awesome aspects. Many in our societies who are still in fear are having problems with these new children because they have not connected with those parts of themselves, which are represented by these children. We need to nurture these beautiful souls and know that they are, in fact, ourselves. Mankind tends to be afraid of what he does not understand. These children are crying out to us to change those outmoded, outdated ways of seeing reality, which are no longer appropriate. They only know of the Oneness and they are here to teach humanity of that oneness. We must be careful not to teach them of the separateness and materialism that have satiated our experience here.

The struggle between male and female, self-consciousness and sub-consciousness is being unified in the influence of Absolute Unity of the Fool. Because of the ability for abstract reasoning, developed by the higher mind, and influenced by Mercury, Man can now touch the Absolute. Mankind has reached up to heaven and in response, God is now coming down to man in all His glory.[7]

The average person lives in a disguise. His words say one thing and his inner thoughts say something very different and so he ends up mostly deluding himself. The suffering that mankind endures is self-inflicted and is directly related to the conflicts of his own mind. When the both aspects of consciousness have no concealments from each other, the individual is said to be "without guile" and is now ready to be admitted into the membership of "Spiritual Israel" who are the overcomers. The two aspects of consciousness are different but equal. One does not dominate the other, neither is one better than the other. Each has its own special powers and sphere of operation.

On the reverse path, the function of the self-conscious or masculine aspect of man is observation of the objective world and the gathering of the data. Sub-consciousness or the feminine aspect in us is the connecting link between the self-conscious and the super-conscious or higher self. It is through the agency of this feminine aspect that a connection is made with the Higher Self or the inner teacher for correct interpretation of the data collected by the observer or masculine aspect of the Self. Without this well- established triangular connection, for establishing confirmation from the Higher Self of the data collected, Mankind continues to operate on misguided information that is interpreted by his sense perceptions. To give us a better understanding of the communicated information to man, we will look at the masculine and feminine symbols in Qabalah so that we can understand the information or divine laws to be collected and interpreted by these two modes of consciousness. Without this correct understanding, we cannot succeed in the Aquarian Age.

The first masculine symbol is that of The Magician and a wise man in contrast to the Fool who stands on the top of a mountain, which is outdoors. He stands in a garden, which might be seen as an ancient form of a house. The Magician or this mode of self-consciousness is represented by the number One and symbolizes the beginning of creation as well as that phase of human affairs, which takes place indoors. He is, therefore, concerned with the family life or the inner world of the individual and the planet. Important to the data collecting activity of the Magician is a table centered in the middle of the garden on which lie four implements all of which are his tools. They are ready and available for use as and when needed. Of great significance is that he stands with a wand uplifted in his right hand pointing to the sky. With his left hand he makes the universal gesture of attention by pointing his extended forefinger toward the fertile earth at his feet.

The Magician is that mode of consciousness, which pays attention, is aware, makes plans and has a grasp on the problems of daily life. As a wise man he sees with his mind's eye and knows the mental function of concentration. The message gleaned from his stance is that the aspirant should be alert and aware and that one's primary concern should be to relate himself to that Source of power, which he is directing from a higher level. Another important concept to grasp is that the aspirant is a transformer and transmuter of the energy that flows through him. Because force flows through us to whatever we give our attention, nothing can escape the mental force of one who has mastered the art of concentration. Concentration is achieved by developing the ability to see through and into things rather than merely looking at them.[8]

The garden to which self-consciousness is directed is subconsciousness and is the place of the hidden powers in man. The four lilies and the five roses symbolize these hidden powers. The four lilies represent varying aspects of truth and indicate that all human

107

knowledge falls in four basic categories. Those four categories of knowledge are symbolized by the four implements on the Magician's table: the wand or the element of fire, the cup or the element of water, the sword or the element of air and the coin or money symbolic of the element of earth.[9]

The five roses represent the five senses and the medium through which all desires are experienced. These lilies and roses in the garden must be tended and carefully improved. By the force of self-conscious control, the aspirant's conscious awareness can take these powers far beyond the limits of natural progression. He is in fact the one who, through careful observation, is able to perceive the underlying principles involved in what is observed. Using these principles, he is then able to apply them to transform his environment and create new realities.[10]

The first tool he uses is the wand, which is an extension of the forefinger and represents the element of fire or the concept of original "ideas." By carefully focusing the attention on the problem and by having a proper relationship with the Source on the higher-level, insight is gained. The aspirant then becomes the medium through which the divine idea is communicated to him. Ageless wisdom has always known that the solution to any problem lies in the problem itself and can only be grasped through clear and focused attention and observation.

The second tool is the cup, which represents the element of water and the quality of emotion or feeling. The cup can be seen as a "shaper" of things and therefore in this next phase of the magical operation he is shaping the ideas formulated in the first phase. After collecting the data or ideas and shaping them he must take action. Without action nothing is ever achieved and nothing can be changed and without action he will never accomplish the realization of his ideas. This is the function of this third implement the sword, which represents the element of air and the quality of mind. Through this mental process he is able to decipher and delineate what is necessary and what is not in the construction of the final product or manifestation. It is important to note that all effective action requires something old or outworn to be torn down and replaced with something new because a principal tool of civilization is controlled and wisely directed destruction.

The result of the action of the previous three produces the fourth, the coin, which is a symbol for money and the element of earth. It also alludes to the fact that all of man's ingenuity has value and all ideas must be realized in form if they are to be of service to man. There are two approaches toward money that must be healed in consciousness in order that money can be available in abundance for humanity's welfare. They are the lust and greed of money by one group and the disdain for money by the other. Until both groups develop a healthy attitude toward this divine energy called money, financial imbalance continues and universal prosperity is delayed. The design on the coin is that of the upright pentagram, the symbol of man in his five-fold expression. Mankind has been living with the reversed or inverted pentagram, which is that of matter dominating spirit, and this is responsible for his incorrect relationship to money.[11]

The sub-conscious response to the Magician is the High Priestess. The Hebrew word for the High Priestess is Gimel meaning camel and a reference to travel. We indicated earlier that the fundamental function of the subconscious is to carry out the will of super-consciousness. When the personality is fused with the soul, as a united vehicle, the communication with super-consciousness becomes possible.

The number two gives us the idea of the function and relationship between one thing and another and in this case, the travel from the beginning of any journey to its end. The High Priestess is also indicating that it is through the increased travel, symbolizing this New Age, that racial, cultural and consequently spiritual unity will be achieved. She sits between two pillars, one black and one white, spirit and matter. She holds the scroll or a book that is a record of the past. We are told in the book of revelation that toward the end of the Piscean Age the book will be opened and the seals removed. It was subconsciousness in the form of Eve who took humanity on the journey into form. She, in the form of Venus-Urania, now a wise-woman, is now the most qualified to take humanity home by opening the book. The truth about the Fall of mankind led by Eve will finally vindicate the feminine aspect of the trinity. When the scroll is read or decoded the true relationship of man to woman will be known and understood. The ideas of separation based on the belief of one race or sex being superior or inferior is caused by the veiled conditions of humanity.

The High Priestess is symbolized by the Moon, which has veiled Vulcan and Uranus. The planet Vulcan, called the forger of metals, is the major influence for impact on man's involutionary journey by breaking through matter so as to deposit divine consciousness in the density of the mineral kingdom, at the same time acting as the veil for this activity.[12] On the evolutionary journey the Moon became the lens for the evolutionary path of return because the basic power of subconscious is memory. She presents us with a method for the retrieval of data through the application of the laws for grouping together mental images in our subconscious filing system. She tells us that the path of evolution is one of remembering. The ability to apply the divine laws for the correct interpretation of reality is of critical importance.

The Moon is the planetary ruler of the sign of Cancer and is the influence under which humanity came into being. In order to understand the great body of knowledge contained in the human form, we must consider the fact that the human form contains data carried forward out of the universal subconscious substance or water by means of the evolutionary process. Mankind emerged out of the waters of life carrying within him the divine ember. He has journeyed through the world of form inhabiting many different bodies, in all of the kingdoms. He is emerging into the fifth kingdom preceded by his journey through the mineral, vegetable, animal and human kingdoms. Mankind's interconnectedness within and through these kingdoms is contained in her scroll and now ready to be deciphered. During this age, humanity will become even more eager to know his heritage and will apply the laws of subconscious to reveal this knowledge, which lies within him.

The first law is that of being alert and aware of what is going on around us and to be totally present at all times and be in the moment. It is also very important to be quiet, relaxed and in a state of receptivity so that the information one desires can rise to the surface. The very idea of what one wants to remember triggers a response from the subconscious; this process requires that clear and precise images must be given. The second law is that of association. The two pillars between which the High Priestess sits give us a clue to remembering. The pillars though opposite in color are the same in shape. When one thinks of dark, there is an automatic thought of light; similarity and contrast, therefore, are the two aspects of the second law of association.[13]

The third law is recency. We tend to remember the things that occurred most recently in our lives. The high priestess does not have to refer to the scroll she holds in order to know what she has recorded. All past information is always readily available. All the occurrences of our present lives are directly related to our past lives. With careful attention to the problem and the application of the divine laws, the cause can be revealed.

The fourth law she applies is repetition. The more anything is repeated, the greater the ability for recall. The more focused, involved and deep is our participation in the affairs of life, the clearer and more vivid will be our memories. These laws are applied by the high priestess or Moon center in the body, the Pituitary or Master gland, which is exoterically and esoterically known to control the bodily functions. However, it is under the influence and impulses of Mercury, represented in the body by the pineal gland, that the Sun affects the integration of the personality vehicle. This is, in part, the process by which the Bride prepares herself for the marriage with the Bridegroom as spoken of in the Book of Revelation. The Ancient Qabalah teaches us that the Sun and the Moon with the aid of Mercury accomplishes the Great Work, which is the merge of the personality and the Soul.

The Sun that is reflected by Mercury is said to be different in quality at different times in our evolutionary process of development, which has three distinct phases. The first phase of influence was when the Physical Sun was in the sign of Leo and was responsible for the development of the animal soul. At this time the animal soul of man was developed and a great multiplication of form took place. It was this Leo influence which brought humanity into the upright position of having an erect spine and so man was able to stand on his own two feet, as an individual human being so as to chart out his own individual identity.[14]

The second lens through which the Sun impacted the next phase of human development was through Neptune. This influence is responsible for the development of the human soul. This "Heart

Sun" brought the physical or personality vehicle in touch with the Soul. Under the influence of Neptune, the God of reason, which is the higher aspects of Pisces and Cancer, humanity was brought to the level of Soul development. The lower emotional and desire nature of man became transmuted into love and aspiration.[15]

Humanity was being prepared and aligned for the influence of the Great Central Sun through an even clearer lens, that of Uranus, so that he could move into divine consciousness.[16] The Moon has veiled the planet Vulcan, the planet responsible for the development of humanity in its earlier stages and the planet Uranus for development into the advanced spiritual man.

Ancient Wisdom tells us that the Moon is in fact dead matter and has no light of her own but reflects the light of the Sun she hides. Many veils are being removed literally and symbolically and as this continues, much of what humanity perceived to be absolute reality will give way to a deeper and clearer understanding of a more accurate reality. The journey of consciousness is an open-ended one and one cannot perceive a reality for which one has not yet developed the capacity to understand and grasp.

We are experiencing much turmoil in our societies, especially from our elders who are watching the collapse of all the systems that have given them a sense of security over the past centuries. What is more accurate is that this change was always taking place but because it was so subtle it was not so apparent or felt by them.

Humanity has been so caught up in the act of surviving on the planet that he did not notice that the appropriate amount of attention was not being given to what was the true reason for his being here. The fact is these changes were always a part of the divine plan, and are happening, right on schedule. Humanity had not been paying attention; he was not allowing the Magician or self-conscious aspect of himself to be applied to his total life as a whole unit. The new children are here to help us grasp a more expanded and exalted understanding of the relationship between spirit and matter. They are helping humanity to reach the zenith of monetary satiation while the Spiritual Hierarchy stays in the background and watch mankind fill himself up until it nauseates him, then he begins to seek something more fulfilling. These new seeds on the planet are helping humanity to understand the ancient wisdom regarding money. From this depth of material satiation, the only place to go is home to one's spiritual Self. When the right understanding of this energy of money is grasped, it will be manipulated for the good of all. Because there is no insufficiency in the abundance of all things, the evolving consciousness will reflect the prosperity that is rightly ours. As humanity is creeping out from under the weight of matter he is beginning to get a glimpse of the future promise. He is, however, afraid to leave behind the comfort he has become accustomed to even though it is outworn and outmoded and does not truly satisfy him any longer. The path of evolution on which all life is based dictates that all things are in constant motion and ever moving toward a more perfect expression of itself. The Moon, the symbol for material form, is exposing the hidden realities of Vulcan and Uranus now that we have a more mature emotional and cognitive humanity. Vulcan influences the less developed and Uranus the more advanced disciple. Mankind will come to better appreciate money once its true nature is revealed and understood.

On the soul level or esoterically, the planet Vulcan is the ruler of Taurus and as we said earlier it is the forger of metals. In respect to humanity it works in the densest, most concrete expression of the natural world. 'Vulcan descends into the depth of matter to find the material needed and applies his art at fashioning that, which is beautiful and useful in humanity.'[17] The exoteric ruler of Taurus is Venus, which is associated with beauty and artistic expression.

We might remember that Taurus is a fixed earth sign and is the sign in which matter is most dense but this is the sphere where base desire moves through form into illumination. So the work of Vulcan on the inner or soul level is to fashion the form aspect of the life in order to bring forth the beauty of the soul. As a destroyer force and aligned with the energy of the First Ray of Will and Power, Vulcan together with Venus had direct impact on the direction of the two World Wars. Vulcan establishes the relationship between humanity and the mineral kingdom and it does so under the control of the human mind. Vulcan influences the aspirant by reaching down to the depth of his being. He is forced to reason out and make correct meaning of Vulcan's destructive action on the crystallized erroneous ideas he holds. This is the influence of Vulcan at the aspirant's first initiation. Mankind has used the mineral kingdom against his fellow men through the use of iron, copper, gold, steel, and other metals in the making of weapons. In conjunction with each other, Vulcan and Venus have established the relationship of man-to-man and nation- to-nation. Through their combined influences these two planets brought humanity out of the depth and caves of concretion. The effects of the horrors of the World Wars brought humanity as a whole to a place within himself where he is now ready to move consciously out of his prison of isolation and separation and into unity and oneness. Mankind began to see and understand that all things are of the One Thing; and that which is perceived as evil, used in the hands of the Master craftsman, fashions a thing of beauty. He is beginning to grasp the subtle distinction between the pairs of opposites and the true relationship between the subtle subjective world and the concrete objective world. This work of Vulcan and Venus ends in the production of the Hierophant, the illumined Man we call the Adept, the Pope or God- Man. The great interplay between the Sun and the Moon aided by Mercury is the dance of life between all the aspects of reality with one aim, the liberation of spirit bound in matter.

From out of the Moon's illusory influence, the work of Vulcan has brought humanity out into the light of first Vulcan, and now Uranus and in union with Neptune through the medium of Mercury. The Moon, which is the exoteric ruler of the personality or form, presides over the death of personality control, as it surrenders to the will of the Soul. Thus is accomplished the long sought after goal of the completion of the Great Work, the merge of the Soul and the personality, and thus a home for the in-dwelling Christ.

The next stage is the fusion of the soul-infused personality with the Monad or spirit, directly. Mercury facilitates this process with the force of energy coming from the Great Central Sun. Mercury has functioned as the messenger of God to man in the person of the Soul. It can be seen that, through the esoteric symbolism of the fluidic nature of quicksilver, the planet Mercury is the link between the more solid nature of personality and the etheric nature of Spirit. Mercury completes its work in humanity when the Soul/personality entity becomes a divine monadic entity.

In the sign of Virgo, the planet of Mercury is both the natural ruler and the planet of exaltation. In this sign, Virgo, the Divine Mother, reveals the essential identity of the Son with the Father; and with Mercury and the Great Central Sun, Uranus.[18] This is the "White Sun" of Absolute Unity as opposed to the "Yellow Sun" of Leo and Relative Unity. Mercury the Son/Sun of Abstract Mind is fused with the Source Uranus thus completing the journey of the prodigal son who comes back to the Father's house. He is now elevated to a higher position than that held before leaving. He now occupies the position of God/Man qualified to rule in heaven and earth. This is the man who is now ready to serve humanity in the Aquarian Age and will form the new leadership in the Spiritual New World Order. This group of Christed beings will become the High priests to humanity so as to lead all life back to the "Father's House".

We are told in the Bible that man, normal man, is not able to see into the face of God. We now understand that it is the stages in the evolution of consciousness, which must occur within the being through the journey of his evolution, which unfolds the capacity to "see the face of God." To his wonder he will discover that he had been looking for himself; it was He all along who was the Great Mystery.

Humanity is now on the verge of a great planetary initiation. We stand at the Eleventh Gate, that of the Aquarian Consciousness, at the dawn of this New Age. When we contemplate the sign of Aquarius and its ruler Uranus, the planet of sudden and unexpected changes, we know what to expect in all areas and departments of human living. We will de-mystify the ancient mysteries and set ourselves free from the bondage of fear, lack and inadequacy.

Most of mankind has felt for ages that there is a small group of souls who have kept the secret truths from the rest of humanity. Because consciousness is the basis for every level of reality that one lives, it follows that perceptions can only change as knowledge increases. Increase in consciousness then, is in direct proportion to knowledge gained. Isis does not unveil herself to the uninitiated; for every man is paid his just wages. One cannot hope to reap what he has not sown. The Scriptures make reference to the fact that anyone who seeks to enter the gates of heaven but who has not come the "straight and narrow way" is a thief and a robber; in other words everyone must walk the razor's edge.

The reason why humanity has been held in captivity has been due to his fear of change, which is the fear of leaving his physical, mental and emotional place of comfort. He has had an unconscious need to be directed, instead of directing himself and taking full responsibility for his destiny. He has projected the leadership of his life onto personalities who he has imbued with, from his perspective, abilities and knowledge he has convinced himself he is unable to possess.

Mankind has been in the process of developing the personality level of his being. His personality level suffers from distortions in consciousness and one of the main aspects of this distortion is separation. This mental separation gives the illusion that one group or person is better than the other, higher or lower than the other and so differentiates all the pairs of opposites with which he deals in his daily life. We must remember, the two pillars of the temple represent the template for this duality and polarization. It is this thinking which has conditioned the personality experience we have lived out on planet Earth.

There have always been a few clever ones in any group who see how they can capitalize on the ignorance and fear of the majority. The few, suffering from their own fear, conclude that there was not enough substance and self-worth to go around so they needed to find a way to acquire and keep as much of everything they could. These few also concluded that if they made these things and anything else important everyone would want them. This they decided was the way to keep humanity on a leash. Likewise, there is a group of souls who have never forgotten their divinity. These are the Starseeds who came into the planet as conscious beings and never lost the consciousness of their divinity. They knew the drama that would be played out on Earth between ignorance and knowledge. They maintained their links with the planets of their origin and became the link to help guide humanity back home. They never allowed themselves to become too mesmerized by the illusions of this planet. They work silently and without much notice, fanfare or money and under great sacrifice to personal comfort they work to insure humanity's conscious return.

As mankind has evolved the capacity of his mind and his heart, he is increasingly realizing that these two groups represent the two aspects of his own nature; that we have played these roles in our changing lives and in our many incarnations. This is the reality of the many masks we have worn. In this New Age, we are moving out of form into formlessness and so Spirit instead of materiality will be the definition for what is important. This new reality requires that each one must know and love him/herself for who s/he really is.

The ability to truly see will become more developed so that the real and the unreal will be more readily discerned. Sight, as defined by ancient wisdom, is the ability to comprehend; this requires the penetration into the very nature of a thing and not merely what seems apparent on the surface.

The secrets that will continue to be revealed will be a function of the veils now falling away from the eyes of humanity. The evolution of sight has taken us through the phases of instinct, intellect, intuition, and finally inspiration.[19] The higher levels of intellectual development have now brought humanity to the intuitional phase and his ability to "hear". Inner sight and inner hearing are next in the higher order of knowing and true comprehension. Pure reason, the ability to see on concrete, logical, rational and abstract levels, allows the aspirant to "hear" the inner teacher. He who has not developed the ability to reason effectively cannot hear his inner teacher who is his only source of life and knowledge. Most fears are based on irrational and illogical conclusions based on what appears to be true.

The influence of Uranus on humanity in the Age of Aquarius is that the will-to-be, and the will- to-know, will become a reality on all levels of manifestation, simultaneously. The veil will be removed from Masonry, which is an ancient and glorious vehicle of knowledge. Masonry, as it has been expressed, is a distortion of what the White Lodge on Sirius intended it to be. Masonry began under the sign of Gemini, which represents the doorway of duality and choice, which was to form the basis for man's initial development.[20] The sign of Libra presents the next doorway and the next marker for taking the understanding of duality forward. In the quiet contemplation in Libra, the aspirant begins to understand the deep occult meanings of those two pillars in the temple and their true relationship to each other. It is in the eleventh sign of Aquarius, the third doorway, that the true meaning of the two pillars of the temple will become understood and lived out.

At the very core of all issues, from the most minute to the most elaborate, is the concept of relationships. Relationships to which attention, association, recency, intensity and repetition must be applied in order to grasp the true meanings of the symbols involved. The soul communicates in symbolic form and so humanity will come to understand that anything that one sees is only a symbol. For everything that is seen there are many, many levels of interpretation on many levels and planes of consciousness. It must not be forgotten that the two pillars, as with any two ideas, naturally give rise to a third. All things are either male or female in nature and are in an eternal sexual, creative exchange with each other and must give birth to a third "something." We have had much experience with duality for eons of years. Now, we will contemplate those dualities from a higher turn of the spiral or point of view, with the idea of creating consciously and constructively. From a consciousness of inclusion and equality, we can make Aquarius the age of manifestation of all our desires for the benefit of all. The middle pillar in the temple is where all humanity meets.

The Black Lodge and the White Lodge are the two governing heads of what many see as the two opposing forces of dark and light battling for control over our planet. The key to the liberation of mankind lies in the resolution of these two forces, first in his thinking, and consequently in his actions.[21] Whatever we run away from will always chase after us because everything seeks to be owned. At the core of every atom is the knowledge of 'the One and from the One.'

One of the laws given to us by subconscious for the revelation of information is that of achieving a state of quietness. Until the fighting is over and the disciple is ready to "hear" the inner teacher, only then will the teacher speak. The disrobed image of the High Priestess indicates that, when the aspirant is ready and still, she will unveil herself to him. In the stillness we must be able to contemplate and reason backward to the source and the nature of the conflict.

We were given the symbol of the Fool as Key "O" the source from which all things in manifestation issued. It is the egg and container of the two forces we call dark and light, negative and positive, female and male and it is, therefore, the originator of the black and the white pillars. All life splits into its two component parts in order to manifest form.

When the Spirit or Primal Fire entered into form, it was carried into the densest of matters, the mineral kingdom. This is symbolic of the Southwest corner of the Lodge that the candidate stands when he enters for initiation. In this symbolic place he is devoid of memory of his place of origin, which is the East. Because of this amnesic state, man has forgotten his own true nature and origin and has commenced to fight against himself. He has forgotten that if he identifies himself with the black or white pillar at the exclusion of the other pillar, he has merely negated one-half of himself.

To legitimize the division of the two lodges, each group sets up its own government, and so the Black Lodge was born with its attendant personnel. It came into existence by those who felt that they were "good" and wanted nothing to do with those who were not as "good" as they were. We, therefore, have mirror images of each other bathing in denial and functioning in extremes. Since we are the co-creators, we have all created the realities we now enjoy. One only has to look at one's own creation to know that the premise from which we have created our present reality must be faulty, and that is why our peace is deferred.

What seems to be at the heart of our dilemma is the absence of conscious participation of the feminine principle in the decision-making process on planet Earth. The unequal representation of conscious divine feminine intelligence in the creation of policies is ludicrous in the extreme. The distortion we see in our present day Masonry reflects this imbalance. This conflict then begs greater insight into the true meaning of the two pillars. They represent the aggregate of man's opposing thought-forms built up over millions of years. This feeling of separation, which is the basis of all evil, has now peaked, and humanity is feeling the urge for Oneness.

The White Lodge on Sirius is the center from which the currents of energy are felt and manipulated for stabilization on this planet. It is the goal of this Cosmic body that the feminine aspect of Deity, whatever form it takes, be restored to her former power and glory.[22] What must become a reality here is that the true knowledge of the "black pillar" and all that it symbolizes must be revealed. As man continues to unfold the knowledge of who he is, and the perception of fear the black pillar symbolizes; this fear must be transmuted into knowledge. The direction of North in the Lodge and the aspirant's life is the place of fear, separation, bondage, ignorance and man's unenlightened state; this is where the black pillar stands. This northern gate holds the promise in the Aquarian Age for the revelation of the secrets it holds. This unveiling will bring about man's liberation.

Uranus, the ruler of the Aquarian Age, is the planetary influence, which will bring occult consciousness to the planet; it is intelligent fusing which produces the scientific atonement of the two factors of light and dark, higher and lower. It does so through the intelligent use of the mind. The scientific revelation of our common genetic origin will provide the framework for the dissolution of the barriers, which have kept our races and nations apart. Under the influence of Uranus we have seen an explosion in new communication, technology and travel. Mankind is now able to travel globally faster both virtually and physically. The world-wide-web simulates the web of life that is the container of life impulses. The grid that held the consciousness of separation is rapidly collapsing and has been replaced by the new template of Oneness. No longer will separation and hate be tolerated here and those for whom this new vibration seem foreign, they will, "will" themselves to another home more appropriate to a vibration expressing the illusion of separation.

The Seventh Ray of Ceremonial Law and Order that works through Uranus is the transmitter of the Sirius force through Pisces to the Spiritual Hierarchy. From the Hierarchy, this force passes to the group of disciples, aspirants and workers whose hearts and hands are committed to the heavy task of the re- organization and the re-building of this shattered world structure.[23]

Djwahl Kuhl describes the Seventh Ray as the "Ray of Ritualistic Decency." It is under this ray that a new world order will be inaugurated, one that is based on spiritual drive, aspiration, mental freedom, loving understanding and a physical plane rhythm which provides opportunity for full creative expression.[24]

Chapter Five

The New World Order - The Spiritual Hierarchy

*Five Sunflowers: Symbols for the four kingdoms and
the emerging fifth kingdom*

Since the earliest beginnings of human life in matter, when Man was still in his deepest sleep, the Hierarchy from the office of the Christ sounded the tone and note that would awaken mankind out of his long sleep. Out of the depth of matter he awoke, bringing with him the faintest embers of remembrance so that his physical apparatus would allow him to register more and more information of quality. Man, the Third aspect of the Supernal Triad, has always been on a data gathering adventure through matter under the supervision and guidance of his initiating First aspect, the Father, through the Hierarchy.

The Sun projected mankind out onto his sevenfold journey into his involutionary journey, into matter. Now, under the sevenfold expression of the Sun, mankind has been making his evolutionary journey back to the Sun, out of the depth of form. Through seven rounds, seven civilizations and seven root races and sub-races, humanity will eventually complete his journey home. This adventure has taken place under the direction and administration of Sirius, where the plan, for the descent and ascent, is kept guarded and executed under the great and capable leadership of the Great White Lodge.[1]

Man is expected to gain an expanded knowledge of himself that only the journey into his own creation can provide. This experience allows man to be the creator and the created of his own reality. As he journeys back, he increasingly regains knowledge of his original nature. The Sirius agenda sets forth the goal for man's understanding of himself through the relationships and associations of the pair of opposites. To achieve this feat mankind must, with each round of emanation, develop higher and higher states of consciousness. This kind of achievement requires the development of his mental faculties. This objective requires mankind to institute certain ways of learning ranging from the crudest to the most advanced and sophisticated methods we now have available today. The direction for this unfoldment has always been under the direction of the Lodge on Sirius where aspects of himself reside in etheric forms.

The first glimmer of mental activity, the ability to make sense of and define the events of his life, came about during the latter part of the third civilization called the Lemurian civilization. The third of the seven civilizations is analogous to the third of the seven levels of consciousness through which mankind must pass. Not much is known of the first two civilizations; I would presume that mankind being completely immersed in matter, remained in a mental fog for a period which is known as the incubation of consciousness in matter.[2]

The Lemurian civilization was an extensive one covering almost the entire then known world, which now lie under the Pacific and Indian oceans. The mental development of mankind in the latter part of this root race saw the emergence of intelligence and later intellectualism. The remnants of the civilization of Lemuria became the transition group that made up the majority of the Atlantean civilization, which emerged after the destruction of the Lemurian continent by fire, eons of years ago.[3] By the beginning of the Fourth Root Race and the Atlantean civilization, its inhabitants had become truly human, completely terrestrial and immersed into matter. He was quite different from his Lemurian predecessor who was said to have been more divine and ethereal.[4]

The Creator Force, which is neither bad nor good when expressing its differentiated aspects in nature, assumes one or the other character. This same differentiation of opposites will eventually lead the intelligent mind to the knowledge of the origin of the dual and triple natures of man: his dual nature is male and female and his triple aspects are Spirit, Soul and Body.

The mental state of Man in his early stage was mindless and animal because the divine spark or fire, which is in all things, was latent in him. It was not until the Monad from the higher spheres incarnated in him and endowed him with understanding, that the ability to reason and to make choices became activated. Prior to this activation, man evolved through the potential inherent in him and all matter. That is to say, he follows the path of evolution through each round and each kingdom.

What separates the animal from human is the activation of the three higher principles of mind: intellect, intuition and inspiration.[5] The development of the mind was achieved at the end of the Third Root race by an upward movement out of the density of matter or water; a process which is symbolized by the upward pointing triangle of the six-pointed star called the hexagram. Corresponding with this is the downward movement of the divine Fire, which is symbolized by the descending triangle. This divine fire imbued the animal-man with higher consciousness, which put him into the Fourth Root Race at the beginning of the civilization of Atlantis; which is reported to be in the areas covering the bed of the Atlantic Ocean.[6]

With the development of the mind and imbued with higher consciousness, humanity's mental eye of understanding was now opened. This led to his identification with the "All" and his oneness with the One Universal Deity. At this point he is feeling within his being, his inner Godhood and of being Man-God even though he is animal in his physical Self. The struggle between these two aspects of his nature began the very day he tasted of the Tree of Wisdom; and thus began a struggle for life between the spiritual and the psychic, and between the psychic and the physical. In the war that ensued, those who conquered the lower principles by obtaining mastery over the body joined the "Sons of Light." Those who fell victim to their lower natures became the slaves of Matter. From the place of being "sons of light and wisdom", they ended by becoming the "sons of darkness." They had fallen in the battle of mortal life, with life immortal, and all those so fallen became the seed of the future generation of Atlantis.'[7]

The earliest Atlanteans on the Lemurian continent separated into the righteous and the unrighteous. That is, those who worshiped the one unseen Spirit of nature and those who worshipped fanatically the Spirits of the Earth, the dark Cosmic Powers with whom they had made alliance. Herein lies the mystery of Cain and Abel; Cain offered sacrifices to the god of matter, but Abel offered them to the life essence within matter. This division in concept evolved into the two groups that became the Lords of Darkness and the Lords of Light.[8] It was in these early times that Thoth also called Hermes, the Thrice Great, began to make his presence felt in the mental development of the Lemuro-Atlanteans. He introduced writing, science, astronomy and medicine with which self-consciousness developed. With the advancement in consciousness, mankind thought himself deeper and deeper into separation. He was now able to see the contrasting aspects of the One and out of this knowledge of the opposites emerged many religious thoughts. Mankind had not yet the ability to understand the connectedness of those aspects of the One Reality. Mankind had now "Fallen" out of the "Oneness" into separateness and thus began the debasement of the Spirit. Pride, lust and rebellion, which had not existed before physical conscious man appeared, now became rampant. Man allowed and nurtured in his heart the development of these demons. Ultimately it is man, therefore, who must redeem himself through the acquisition of higher knowledge.[9]

During the early Lemurian times when instinct and desire were identical, man was provided for in the Garden of Eden. When he developed the ability to reason and to contemplate the separate aspects of the One, he reasoned that he must be able to provide for himself. After the Fall from grace, Man was then symbolically cast out of the Garden of Eden and thus he was forced to contrive ways of taking care of himself. His powers of acquisition and his desire for material things began to grow through his ability to set goals and achieve those goals.[10]

Man's nomadic way of life gave way to a community form of living and the development of agriculture that contributed to a more material and comfortable way of life. As the need to acquire material possessions grew, so did his sexual indulgences and the expansion of his families. Out of all of this came the development of a large welfare state. The Priest-Kings of the day made up the Intelligentsia and they possessed great scientific knowledge which made them appear as gods to the masses. These members of the Hierarchy, who stayed in the background, brought about great developments in transportation, sanitation, hygiene, and air machines. They had the ability to control the air and the waters through manipulation of the forces of nature and the four elements. These sophisticated advancements were not the result of the systematic development of the minds of the Atlanteans, but rather was a gift to them by the Hierarchy. The technological developments of our day are and will continue to be the manifestations of the ideas and ideals held out to humanity in the days of Atlantis by the Hierarchy. In our time we are seeing and will continue to see the magnificent concrete manifestations of those ideals in all the fields of human endeavor.[11]

The division of knowledge between these two groups created an even wider gulf between the Priest- Kings and the masses and this division finally culminated in a great war between those who became the Forces of Darkness and the Forces of Light. The Great Flood brought the war on Atlantis to an abrupt end under the influence and intervention of inter-planetary forces. A remnant of that civilization which was saved in Noah's Ark, constitute the seed group of the Fifth Root race to which Europe is host.[12] It was a state of immature development based on emotional and physical priorities, which necessitated their destruction. This immaturity was evident in man's control and subjugation of the sub-human kingdoms and elemental forces of the planet. The problems of our time are direct outgrowths of the problems on the Atlantean continent.[13] Lest humanity loses heart, it must be remembered that behind all of the drama of human unfoldment, the "Hierarchy" stands. The elder brothers and masters of the race can be found guiding humanity satisfactorily along the path of life and evolution to his present point of development. The three Planetary Centers from which the governance of humanity and life, in general, is conducted are: Shamballa, the Hierarchy and the Center of Humanity; they function together as a triune force, yet with specific energies of expression.[14]

Shamballa is the Planetary Head Center and focuses its energy through the spiritual pineal gland. It is called the Holy City and is the center of Will or Power from which the Purpose or Plan for all life comes. The Ruler of this center is the Ancient of Days, Melchizedek. In the past, the force from this center would reach humanity through the Hierarchy of Masters due to the inability of man's vehicle to accommodate this intensity of energy. This is no longer the case since man has evolved greatly in his physical, emotional and mental bodies. Shamballa is now for the first time making its impact on humanity directly. Many First Ray souls who are automatically attuned to the Shamballa force are here under certain karmic agreements to bring forward and work out their salvation with humanity for the final liberation of all.[15]

The crises on Lemuria, Atlantis, both World Wars and all major and minor wars are evidences of the forces of Shamballa making its presence felt by creating opportunities to shatter the illusion of separateness in the consciousness of man. On these dramatic occasions, the Dweller on the Threshold, which controls the Law of Polar Opposites, meets the Angel of the Presence and this brings about the attainment of Planetary Initiation.[16]

The second planetary center is the Hierarchy or Heart Center of Love and Wisdom. It works in conjunction with Shamballa to carry out the Plan and purpose on behalf of humanity. The Hierarchy is concerned with Group Consciousness and the concept of Unity. The etheric center for the Hierarchy is the New Jerusalem and the place where the temple not made with hands is symbolically built. Its spiritual Ruler is the Christ who is also the World Savior.[17]

The third planetary center of Active Intelligence and Creativity is that of Humanity focusing through the Throat center. It is the self-conscious aspect of Divinity whose Ruler is Lucifer, Son of the Morning, and is the representative, Prodigal Son.[18] In the system of the Qabalah, these three planetary centers are under the names of Ehyehe, Hod-Heh-Vav-Heh and Elohim and are the outer vehicles for the three Veils of the Absolute, Ain, Ain Suph and Ain Suph Aur.

The Hierarchy of Masters is that which works directly with humanity as head of the seven great departments of life, which corresponds to and influences all the departments of our temporal systems. On the first ray is Master El Morya who works closely with the institutions of law, politics and government through the agency of his disciples and Initiates who are also on the first ray. His goal is to bring about right human relations, and in the production of that synthesis of effort, create a new intuition. This will bring about a changing political consciousness and environment in which the family of nations can stand together for the basic values of:

1. Freedom of the individual

2. Right international interplay which will finally bring about the end to all wars and

3. Clean political regimes free from selfish ambition and dirty political maneuvering. To this end, all statesmen in all countries who are receptive are impulsed toward the achievement of these goals.[19]

Under the leadership of the second Ray which is Master of Education and Religion, Master Kuthumi, his disciples and Initiates work with Master El Morya in the education of the general public toward truer values. The goal is that of a trained and enlightened public who can shoulder right responsibilities and who will elect men and women whose vision are in line with the ethics and science of right human relations. This public will recognize as a basic political tenet that which is defined as the equality of all men founded on basic and universal divinity.[20] His department is responsible for the spiritualization of mankind; therefore, his work extends to the heads of all religious organizations and all those who are preparing humanity for the re-appearance of the Christ through better spiritual understanding of the purpose and plan for all humanity. The sixth ray of Religion and the fourth ray of Harmony through Conflict as well as the even rays come under the broad direction of the Master of the Second Ray. Most of the incarnated souls are of this ray of Love and Wisdom and it is to them that the work of reconstruction and rebuilding has been naturally committed. Only through education, which teaches the true relationship between the heart and the mind can harmony be achieved and conflict end.[21]

The third planetary department is under the leadership of Count St. Germaine, also called Master Rakozci. He is the hierarchical representative in Europe who is also the Lord of Civilization. Those disciples and initiates who stand with him are those who have passed the tests under the conditions of the previous two rays. They are now ready to stand with that unbreakable and immovable determination that says a situation shall be handled and so whatever is needed for the liberation of mankind must appear. This must and is the quality of intention the disciples now possess.[22] He is preparing the center of Humanity for receptivity to the great influx of energy from Sirius through the

Shamballa center. The activities in the department of business and finance are overseen and directed by Master Rakozci especially in Europe and the United States of America. As the Master also of the Seventh Ray of Ceremonial Law, Order and Alchemy, he works with the masters of the odd rays: ray five, the ray of concrete science and ray one, the ray of law, politics and government to bring in the civilization for which mankind has waited so long. He is intensely involved with the worldwide economic problems and with the transmutation of the basic materialistic obsession of humanity. In this regard he is gathering together and training the capitalists, labor leaders, financial experts and thinking workers and members of all ideologies for the work of preparing men's minds for the return of the Christ and the New Age.[23]

Many of these people in the different departments of life are those who one might call non-spiritual in an orthodox religious sense but they are all highly spiritual in the correct sense. They exemplify within themselves a kind of living that is the hallmark of discipleship. In them are the three factors of right motive: selflessness, service and intelligence, all of which must be present in men everywhere if they hope to be fit for training so as to be able to work with the Hierarchy and be in the service to humanity. These are the men and women who are the hope of the future.[24] Under the united energies of these three planetary centers, the Will of God, the Love of God and the Intelligence of God will fuse and blend on Earth in relation to human problems. The necessary conditions will then be achieved and will set in motion the bringing to an end of all wars as well as economic and educational imbalance and inequity. To this end, it is important to understand the influence of the Jewish people on the evolution of both Matter and Spirit. The Jewish Force is the fourth planetary center and the meeting place of the three divine aspects. The Jew, with his emphasis on being the "chosen people", does not realise that he has been chosen to be the symbolic wandering incarnating soul.[25]

The Jewish people have failed to hold before the world the divine nature of all mankind who are equally divine and are the Lord's elect. When the Jewish people can understand the symbolic mission with which their race was entrusted, and know that the Lord's elect are all the people of the Earth, only then will we have a different world. The fourth planetary force is influenced by the solar plexus chakra and expresses world emotion and sensitivity. This Jewish Force is conditioned by the seventh ray aspect of the Third Ray which influences both magic and money. The Jews are the instruments for the working out of the plan for the production of certain syntheses as well as to bring humanity to certain realizations and decisions. When the mind aspect is fully developed, then the focus of the Dark Forces will change and the problems of the Jews will disappear. The effects of this change will constitute the new Aquarian culture and civilization.[26]

The spiritual Israelites and seed groups have been "esoterically anchored" in the many governmental and private systems of the world. In these groups are those who can respond to the subtler forces. Through the strength of their clear thought they can produce those conditions within the existing world trends and world groups which will enable the new sciences, the new approaches in divinity, the new education, and the new modes of handling the economic situations and the political problems to precipitate and further the growth of the Kingdom of God. This fifth kingdom in nature will then be a tangible, factual and objective reality on Earth.[27]

As discussed in chapter three, the Third Ray conditions the Jewish people astrologically. That is, the Ray of Humanity and the affairs of business, finance and the marketplace. When this energy is expressed on the lower arc we have selfish acquisition, holding and hoarding. Their soul ray is the First, that of Will or Power and that which influences politics, law and government. When the aspects of these rays are expressed on a lower arc we have militancy and the indiscriminate use of the sword. The placement of Virgo in the astrological make up of the Jewish people also sets up an attitude of racial purity and the feeling of being the "chosen people" therefore perpetuating the attitude of separateness. We as a human family must solve the problem with understanding and co-operation and end ancient hatreds and antagonisms. Fusing the problem into one vast humanitarian situation is the only way this can be done.[28]

The problem we call the Jewish problem is the problem of humanity, for the Jews are found in every land. These issues are merely being magnified for us through the "Jewish people." In order for this problem to be solved we must be able to identify and solve the Jewish problem in each of us. When this problem is solved only then will racial fusion and harmony be possible and will we have peace on Earth.

Our planet and this solar system were chosen as the nursery for the seeds of separateness. Why this remnant of humanity should have been destined to work out its future on our Earth is hidden in the knowledge of the Lord of the First Ray, Melchizedek, and this fact will one day be revealed for all to know. Only when the Jewish people accept their role in the problem, by letting go of their own separative tendencies and their sense of persecution by everyone else, can the solution come. Jews and Gentiles alike must take equal responsibility for the world's difficulties. To aid in the transmutation of these planetary issues, the disciples must have a clear understanding of the problems on a causal level and must become pure unclogged channels though which the energies from the Hierarchy and Shamballa can work.[29]

The fifth planetary center is the materialistic force or the matter aspect; it corresponds to the planetary sacral center and it is the conditioning influence in man. The fifth ray aspect of the first ray in nature is the force influencing this center. These five centers relate to the five kingdoms in nature. One of the characteristics of this force at its lowest level of expression is inertia. Inertia expresses itself in many ways in the life of the aspirant such as spiritual cowardice and illegitimate physical ailments preventing them from being involved in the work for the liberation of souls. The fear that people have of speaking of the Kingdom of God to others, for fear that they will be rebuffed, becomes another hindrance to the advancement of the spiritual work. They lose precious opportunities and never discover how ready many souls are for liberation. When aspirants are released from these limiting conditions many more man-hours can be added to the service so that the return of the Christ can be hastened. This inertia must be transmuted into a higher quality of energy upon which the spiritual hierarchy operates.[30]

It is under the direct leadership of the Hierarchy that the responsibility lays for the evolution of all life everywhere. It is to this task that the Master Jesus and Kuthumi have dedicated their existence. This was made possible through the different vibrational forms they have assumed since the beginning of time. The Hierarchy may be defined as the Planetary Center, which is and has been the guiding principle for the evolution of Life on this planet since our advent here. By way of understanding this force, it becomes important to know that the entire hierarchy of spiritual beings is a synthesis of forces or energies, which are manipulated for the furtherance of planetary evolution. These forces operating in our planetary scheme through the great personalities who comprise the Hierarchy link it and all that it contains with the greater Hierarchy of the Solar System. The Hierarchy of this planet is a miniature replica of the greater syntheses of those self-conscious Entities on the Higher Planes. They manipulate, control and demonstrate through the Sun and the seven sacred and non-sacred planets in our solar system.[31]

The Hierarchy has four divisions of work:

1. To provide the appropriate conditions for the development of self-consciousness in all life in all the four kingdoms. It achieves this through man, the macrocosm to the three lower kingdoms. It does this by blending the higher three aspects of Spirit with his lower four. This is achieved through the example mankind sets in service, sacrifice and self-denial, and through the streams of Light, which he occultly emanates. The Hierarchy could be considered as the collective of the forces of the Fifth kingdom on our planet. One enters this kingdom through the full development and control of the fifth principle of mind and its transmutation into wisdom. Through the faculty of discriminative love, this intelligence of the higher mind is applied to all states.

   This love expresses itself through the five kingdoms in nature on an evolutionary arc. The mineral, vegetable, animal, human and spiritual kingdoms all embody this love as some type of consciousness.

2. It is the work of the Hierarchy to develop these types to perfection through the adjustment of karma, the agency of force and by providing the right conditions for the development of consciousness.[32] In the mineral kingdom, the Hierarchy directs itself to the development of discriminative and selective activity. A characteristic of all matter is activity of some kind. At the point when that activity is directed

toward the building of forms, even of the most basic or elemental kind, the faculty of discrimination will be demonstrated. Scientists recognize this as an approximation of divine wisdom.[33] In the vegetable kingdom, which is the rudimentary condition of the second aspect of divinity, this faculty of discrimination is added as a response to sensation. In the animal kingdom, the rudimentary activity of feeling increases and, symptoms of the first aspect of embryonic will and purpose are discernable as hereditary instinct.

It is appropriate therefore that man is considered the macrocosm of the three lower kingdoms, for in him these three lines of development are synthesized so that they come to full fruition. It is in man that intelligence is actively and wonderfully manifested. He is embryonic love and wisdom and in him is the presence of dynamic and initiating will, which come to fuller development when he enters the fifth kingdom.[34]

In the fifth kingdom, group consciousness is developed and leads to the full expression of the Love- Wisdom faculty. As the initiate works as a Master and as part of the Hierarchy, the Love-Wisdom aspect comes to its consummation. At the sixth and seventh initiations the First or Will aspects shine forth and from being a Master of Compassion and a Lord of Love, the adept gradually becomes something more. He enters into a still higher consciousness than that of the group and becomes God-conscious and then, the great Will-Purpose of the Logos becomes his.[35]

3. To transmit the will of the planetary Logos to mankind and all the kingdoms below. It is now the work of those who

have attained this higher consciousness to tend to the seed of self-conscious development in all beings. These members of the fifth kingdom act as transmitters to man, to the devic kingdom, and to angels of the light of synthesis and divine knowledge.

4. To be an example to humanity. As an example to humanity, it is important for aspirants to know that the members of the Hierarchy are those who live as humans, past and present, but have triumphed over matter and achieved the goal of mastery over the senses. These spiritual personalities, adepts and Masters have wrestled and fought for victory on the physical plane. They have struggled with the illusions, fog, dangers, sorrows and pain of daily life. They have trodden every step of the path of suffering and have undergone every experience. They have surmounted every difficulty and emerged triumphant. They now stand symbolically, as does the Hermit, on the top of the mountain that he has climbed, and with the Light, which he is He guides humanity on.[36]

These Elder Brothers of the race have all undergone the crucifixion of the personal self and know that complete renunciation of all is the destiny of every aspirant. There is no phase of agony, no wrenching sacrifice, no Via Dolorosa that they have not in their journey trodden. Their right to serve and the methods they use in service lie in the knowledge and wisdom of this journey.

They know the quintessence of pain and the depth of sin and suffering and because of this knowledge their methods can be perfectly measured to the need of each individual. They are, at the same time, aware of the realization of the liberation to be achieved through pain, penalty and suffering. They have a deep understanding of the freedom that comes through the sacrifice of the form by the medium of the purifying fires. This helps to give them a firm grip on the challenges of various situations. It also gives them the ability to persist even when mankind may seem that they have suffered enough. They have a love that triumphs over all setbacks, for this love is founded on patience and experience.[37]

These elder brothers of humanity are characterized by a love, which endures and acts always for the good of the group. This knowledge is gained through millennia of lives lived in which they have worked their way from the bottom of life and the evolutionary well, to the top. They can be defined through an experience, which is based on time itself and through a multiplicity of personality actions and reactions, as well as courage, which is the result of that experience.

This knowledge, experience and courage have been produced by ages of endeavor, failure and renewed undertakings, which in the long run has led them to triumph. They can now be placed at the service of the race for a purpose that is enlightened, intelligent and co-operative. This service is always adjusting itself to the requirements of the group and the hierarchical plan, thus fitting in with the purpose of the Planetary Ruler.

They are ultimately distinguished by the knowledge of the power of sound. This final fact is the basis of the maxim, which states that all true occultists are distinguished by the characteristics of knowledge, dynamic will, courage and silence. They know well the old occult maxim, which is: "To know, to will, to dare and to be silent." Because by knowing the plan so well and having clear illuminated vision, they can bend their will unflinchingly and unswervingly to the great work of creation by the power of sound. This leads to their silence where the average man would speak and their speaking where the average man is silent.[38]

The Hierarchy of Masters was founded back in the time of the middle of the Lemurian civilization when a great crisis occurred. This was the time that the Ancient of Days Sanat Kumara and six other Kumaras came into the sphere of our dense physical plane and were unable to fully descend into matter. He performed His functions in the etheric body of the planet. With Him came a large group of highly evolved Entities, which form the triple aspect of His Being. They embody the forces of the head, heart and throat centers and came in with Him to form focal points of planetary administration for the helping of the great plan and for the self-conscious unfoldment of all life. As members of the human family evolved they replaced members of the original group who had come in with the Ancient of Days.[39]

The immediate effect of His advent into the etheric plane of our planet is still being felt. The seven centers in the head are linked to the other centers in the body and are analogous to the seven Kumaras. When these seven planetary centers are activated through the center called the seat of the soul in the pineal gland, this energy spreads the force of this energy throughout the body. The head center of the planet and of the body controls the heart and throat centers and consequently controls all the remaining major and minor centers. The entrance of the Ancient of Days to the planet brought about an extraordinary stimulation and a great leap forward for all life. The animal-man moved into the human kingdom; thus radioactivity developed in the mineral kingdom as chemical changes occurred in the vegetable kingdom.[40]

After the descent of the Spiritual Entities, the work for the implementation of the plan on Earth was systemized. Offices were apportioned and the processes of evolution in all the departments of nature were brought under the conscious and wise guidance of this initial Brotherhood. This work continues and is maintained by the Brotherhood of Light who lives here in dense physical bodies and/ or in etheric bodies. It is important for mankind to be aware that these Masters live among us controlling our destinies and guiding the affairs of the planet and by so doing leading its evolution to ultimate perfection.

The work of the Hierarchy stumbled along with success and failures until the middle of the fourth root race on Atlantis when another evolutionary crisis occurred. This required large numbers of the members of the Hierarchy to leave the planet for higher work elsewhere in the solar system and so highly evolved human beings replaced them.[41]

At this time the Council made the following decisions:

1. To close the door through which animal-men passed into the human kingdom.

2. To open another door to permit members of the human family who were willing to go through the necessary discipline and make the required effort to enter the fifth or spiritual kingdom. This allowed the Hierarchy to be drawn from the earth's humanity who was qualified.

3. It was decided that the line of demarcation between the two forces of matter and spirit be clearly defined and so the inherent duality of all manifestations became emphasized. The aim was to teach men how to liberate themselves from the limitations of the fourth or human kingdom into the fifth or spiritual kingdom.

The problem of good and evil, light and dark, wrong and right was enunciated solely for the benefit of humanity so as to enable him to cast off the shackles that imprisoned his spirit. This problem does not exist in the kingdom below man nor for those who transcend the human kingdom; mankind must learn through experience and pain, of the duality in all existence. When man achieves liberation, he finds that indeed all is one. He knows unequivocally that spirit and matter are a unity and that nothing exists outside the Oneness or the great body of the Planetary Logos.[42]

Through the discriminative faculty, which is the distinctive quality in man, the Hierarchy enabled man, through the balancing of the pairs of opposites, to reach his goal and find his way back to the source from which he came. This great struggle to find balance between the Forces of Light and Darkness was characteristic of Atlantis. The World Wars and all the lesser conflicts of our current time are representative of this same struggle. Mankind can understand the events of the present only when a correct perspective is established, since all events of life exist between a past and a projected future.[43]

The point of evolution reached by mankind and the place he now occupies in his evolutionary process, positions him at a doorway which necessitates drastic changes in his entire attitude toward life and world relations. The changes that are occurring are being initiated by him and are not externally imposed. Man is now at the point where the principle of intelligence is strongly awakened within him and nothing can hinder his progress into knowledge. However, this knowledge can be used either for uplifting or destroying humanity, if dangerously misused and selfishly applied or if nothing is done to halt and save him from himself. He must, therefore, be taught to react to a higher sense of values. It is important for the aspirant to know that the whole history of the world is based on the emergence and acceptance of ideas and the transformation of those ideas into ideals. These ideals are later superceded by new and more expansive ideas. These ideas do not originate in the mind of man, but are imposed on the minds of men through his personal and collective oversoul or higher aspect. Man will reach mankind through the form of emanations or impulses, and embody the divine plan for the progress of humanity as well as the planet. Man can either retard or accelerate the progress of the plan by his ability to use these ideas through his understanding.[44]

The Lords of Liberation are those Adepts and Initiates who have come out of the race of man and are themselves an expression of the divine idea. It is through them that the basic urge to freedom and liberation has slowly and consistently dominated human thought and life. It is this that leads first to the struggle for individual freedom and then liberation. This impulse further leads to the ideal of heaven: initiation, spiritual attainment and later to the greater ideal of self-determination. It is to these souls that the charge for the liberation of humanity is given. Once these ideas become ideals, mankind has the option of accepting or rejecting them regardless. However, the plan moves on.[45]

A vast number of humanity has reached a point of integration and are now beginning to function as a unit unto themselves, as a way of preparation for conscious integration into the greater Whole. From the form side, the mind functions through the brain centers to bring the physical, emotional, and mental bodies into unison. At this stage, the higher correspondences of love, wisdom and higher thought must and will appear. The urge by humanity to go forward to higher achievements and to search for that which is better is very strong and the Hierarchy of Love is endeavoring to hasten the process, yet it is always facing the risk of complications.[46]

There are men and women in increasing numbers and from every field of thought who are expressing the potency of their achieved integration. Because of their unfoldment as well as the reality of their soul contact, achieved by emerging out of the level of human, they stand above their fellow humans. Through the force of their personality integration, they can now function as high-grade persons. These individuals in the fields of government, religion, science, philosophy, economics and sociology are having a uniting and powerful effect, some good and some not so good. Though their motives may be sound and good, due to inexperience in the ways of the soul, they make many mistakes and lead many people into error and much trouble. However, in the long run what results is the awakening of the public consciousness, which is always good.[47]

Next is the emergence of a new racial group. This group is forming in every land but especially where Caucasians are found. The fifth or spiritual kingdom is emerging out of the fifth root race, which is all of humanity. The Caucasian race is playing host to this evolutionary phase of the spiritual development of humanity and all life. The new racial type is by far more one of a state of consciousness rather than of a physical form. Invariably, over time, any developed state of consciousness conditions and determines the shape of the body and produces ultimately certain physical characteristics.[48]

Another factor affecting the unrest in the world is the ending of the Age of Pisces that has brought all the Piscean ideals to a point of crystallization or death. The major Piscean ideals were:

1. The idea of authority, which led to the imposition of different forms of paternalism as well as political, educational, social and religious ideologies on humanity.

2. The idea of the value of sorrow and pain; it has been taught to humanity that there are virtues to sorrow and that pain has definite educational value. Thus, humanity has been forced to acquiesce and then, by overdoing it, he has steeped himself in misery. In the new age all this will be swept away in the clear light of love and understanding.

3. In a similar manner the idea of self-sacrifice usually under the coercion and the imposed submission of a stronger will has been the experience for all levels of humanity.

4. The idea of the satisfaction of desire being one of the hallmarks of the Piscean era, has been characterized by material production, commercial expansion and skilled salesmanship. Humanity has been educated to believe that material possessions are essential to their happiness. The Hierarchy of Wisdom has allowed this to continue unchecked for a long time in order to allow mankind to become satiated; however, a revolt in the direction of simplicity is now gaining ground.

5. The effects of the coming into full manifestation of the Aquarian Age making their influences felt in the lives of the human race. The Hierarchy is counting, with assurance that these steady emerging influences will bring a consciousness of universal relationships. This will be the climaxing gift of the period we are now in.[49]

The Aquarian Man will bring into manifestation great ideals because the channel of contact between soul and brain via the mind will be steadily established through right understanding. The Mind will be used increasingly in its dual activity as the penetrator into the world of ideas and as the illuminator of life upon the physical plane.[50] This advancement in conscious evolution now necessitates the externalization of the Spiritual Hierarchy. These Masters of Wisdom will make themselves known and mankind will see and know who these great Beings are. They have watched, nurtured and guided the steady evolution of life for eons.

The Christ, who is the head of the Hierarchy, ascended and withdrew from the planet over two thousand years ago. On his departure, he promised that he would return at the end of the age. There is a deep-seated conviction, innate in the consciousness of humanity that some day some great teacher, a savior, revealer, lawgiver and divine representative must come forth in response to the need and demand of humanity. The time has come, and the appeal of simple faithful hearts has penetrated into the highest spiritual spheres and set in motion, the energies and forces, which cannot now be stopped. The innocent invocative cry of distressed humanity is today of such a volume, sound and pitch that it has, united with the wisdom and knowledge of the Hierarchy and given rise to certain activities from the Father's House or Shamballa. This will result in the transformation of Divine Will-to Good into human goodwill, and resultant peace on Earth.[51]

Preparing humanity for the imminent return of the Christ is the greatest event for which the Hierarchy has been involved, through the steady development of consciousness in humanity. Those among Humanity who can stand with focused intent, strenuous physical service and determined effort, so as to struggle even unto death to defeat evil, will prevail. They must be able to preserve the inner attitude of love and non- separateness, relinquish all for the love of humanity and sacrifice everything for the cause of freedom and righteousness. The forces of cosmic evil are fighting furiously against the externalization of the spiritual work. The channeling of their forces of evil on our plane, are generated through three channels:

1. The center of cosmic evil on the Astral plane which can only be understood by the higher initiates. These forces are negated by the rapid spiritualization of humanity. As the illusion of mankind weakens, so does the potency of the astral plane. The power of cosmic evil will correspondingly weaken and gradually the forces of evil will be unable to reach the planet as easily, any longer. It is against the impact of this force of evil that the Hierarchy stands united in protection of humanity.

2. The Black Lodge is the representative of ancient and cosmic evil on Earth, as the White Lodge corresponds to the Cosmic Center of Light on Sirius. The externalization of the Black Lodge is much more anchored on Earth and the physical plane than is the White Lodge or Hierarchy. This is so because materialism and separateness are the premises on which the Black Lodge is established and continues to function. It is far more difficult for the Hierarchy to clothe itself in matter and walk on the plane of matter than it is for the Black Lodge. Owing to the spiritual growth of mankind and to the steady orientation of humanity to the spiritual hierarchy, the time has come when the Hierarchy can materialize and meet the enemy of good on an even footing. The Hierarchy need not be further handicapped by working in substance while the Evil forces work in both substance and matter. Once the reappearance of the Christ and the Hierarchy is an established fact, there will be a sure defeat of the forces of evil. The Black Lodge or the planetary center of evil, works almost entirely upon the astral plane. It is impressed directly by, and guided in detail, from the cosmic astral plane.

3. The forces of Evil work from the negative or purely material forces of the planet; these are not necessarily bad or good.

However, these forces have been used instinctually and often unconsciously by humanity for purely material ends. They are, therefore, basically anti-spiritual and subject to the influence of human desire. They are also oriented toward selfishness, and inherently towards separateness. Due to a lack of knowledge and understanding, humanity is unaware of the interlocking and inter-penetrating grades of evil and how numerous and intricate they are.[52]

When past illusions have been dispelled, the astral plane will then be illuminated and the mental plane irradiated. Then will come the revelation of new truths of which our present ideals are only signposts. The present demand is for knowers, for those whose minds and hearts are open, and those who are free from great ancient idealisms. These idealisms must now be recognized as only partial indications of unrealized truths. If the lessons of our world situation and catastrophes are duly and truly learned, there are great truths that can be learned for the first time.[53]

The Supreme Head of the Hierarchy will return in this Aquarian Age as Himself, that is, the Water Bearer, in order to meet the needs of the thirsty nations. We know that the peoples of this Earth, thirsty for truth, loving understanding and right human relations are eagerly awaiting that return.

The Rider on the White Horse spoken of in Revelation chapter 19 will return when a measure of peace has been restored, when the principle of sharing is at least in the process of controlling economic affairs, and the churches have begun to clean house. The Kingdom of God will then appear and be publicly recognized, and no longer be a thing of dreams and ideals.[54]

Chapter Six

Man, The Measure of Things

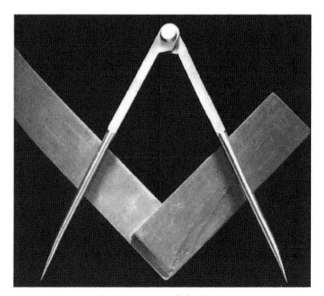

The Compass and the Square

Man is said to be the 'principal phenomenon' of the world because of his ability to penetrate into the mystery of his own nature, and by so doing have the nature of the cosmos revealed to him. By considering himself, man gains an understanding into the reality at the heart of that mystery, which is himself. Man is an actor in the world drama in which he assigns to himself the part he will play in that drama. He is the actor and the producer of that play. He alone can turn the play and his role in it into reality.

Man has taken part in the whole cycle of world creation from the formless beginnings up to its most finely differentiated aspects. He is the settler of his own fate. He fulfils his own destiny while at the same time he must fulfill the fate and destiny of the universe to which he belongs and with which he is one.

The stages of birth, youth, adulthood, old age and death, in all forms in the world, correspond to the stages of man's evolution. The individual man and humanity as a whole have evolved from being merely body to the development of the Soul and then to the development of the Spirit. There is nothing that exists that man does not have a hand in. Says the Hermetic Axiom: 'That which is above, is as that which is below', indicating that man is the measure of all things and at the same time man is the first matter or Prima Materia from which all things in creation issued forth. However, man has become so "intellectual" and "cultured" that he has thought himself into separation from himself, not realizing that he is a part of the Godhead.

Man has been described as a point of divine light hidden within a number of enveloping sheaths or as a light that is hidden within a lantern. That light can be either both bright and radiant and of great use to humanity, or hidden and dark and of no use to others. The light of the soul emerges as, and in proportion to, the intelligent use of the mind in meditation. The soul has been described as one of the greatest mysteries of life. It is the seat of consciousness and is eternal in Man's being. Only by the action of the soul can the breath of human consciousness be changed and be extended to become cognizant of the transcendental world. This evolution of the soul has produced the physical characteristics such as his form and the expressions of his face, color, liveliness and soul-content of his look. Contained in the soul is the knowledge of man's fate, what he is, and what is needed for him to become. It is through and by means of the soul that the total activities during incarnation are balanced with the karmic account. The soul hides within itself the endless possibilities that lie within the endless sea of powers, sensations and thoughts, between birth and rebirth.[1]

It is through the medium of the soul that man gains insight into the totality of experiences into other worlds that lie behind what is available to his limited vision. Ordinary knowledge about earthly things is different from super-natural, super-normal insights and this knowledge is to be attained, not only by means of inborn faculties, but also by the concentration of the totally integrated personality.

The whole man must know, on a cellular level, and not just in his head and in his brain. This occult knowledge penetrates his body, mind and spirit. No one can progress in this knowledge unless his whole attitude is oriented toward higher ideas and views. The more harmony of feeling, thinking and willing is developed by man, the freer he will be and the fewer will be the breaks in the penetration of the divine ray. Only then can the "inner light" of the soul shine. For man to be "happy", he must have full insight into his own nature and right appreciation of the living powers by which his life and those of his fellow men are made more complete.

The full measure of man must be grasped in order for him to appreciate his own awesomeness and responsibilities in relationship to himself and the lower kingdoms in nature. To this end, we will look at the fivefold nature of man through his symbolic structure and function as represented by the five elements of Akasha, Fire, Water, Air and Earth.

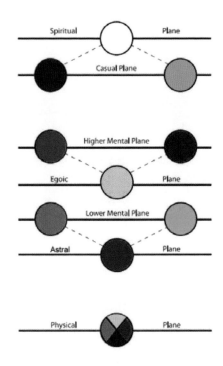

Spiritual   Plane
Casual Plane
Higher Mental Plane
Egoic   Plane
Lower Mental Plane
Astral   Plane
Physical   Plane

The Four Planes on which man is measured and constituted

Kether is the center of conscious radiant energy, which is Living Light. It is from this concentration of energy that all cycles of manifestation spiral out through the ten steps or emanations on the Tree of Life.

Chokmah, the next cosmic principle, is the sphere of the zodiac or the sphere of the fixed stars, and knowing itself to be Light, it radiates this light to stars and suns, which it reflects to planets. This self-knowledge expresses itself as understanding in Binah, to whom is attributed the divine Breath called Neshamah. Binah is the sphere of Saturn. She presides over the special and particularized manifestation of quantity, quality, mass and form.

She is the source of the intuitive knowledge of spiritual truth and is also the source of guidance in the progression of mankind toward mastery. She is the Dark Mother always pregnant with divine ideas to be birthed. In the sphere of Binah is Akasha (Ether), the Astral Light. However, Ether is the lower manifestation of Akasha in our solar system. Akasha is said by occultists to represent, in part, the subtle principle of hearing or sound vibration. It is the all-pervading element, and its characteristic qualities are electricity, magnetism, light, sound, heat, cohesion and cold, and is said to occupy pure space. Out of Akasha, everything came into form and into Akasha everything must return. It is, therefore, called the great mixing bowl of the elements.[2] The Ancients of many cultures tell us that those projections came in the form of sound and as having seven definite rays of energy vibrations. The Cosmic Command or Word is the articulate word of creative power and is what we may call the Holy Spirit. Life in this Creative Word is the origin of all things in manifestation. It was projected into physical manifestation by the power of sound from the Causal Plane of the Supernal Triad: Kether, Chokmah and Binah. The three alchemical principles upon which all creation is built and from which all matter is formed, emanates from this supernal triangle. Binah, the sphere of Active Intelligence, carried out the need for expansion. This creative process initiated the whirling and combining of the alchemical elements of air, water and fire. From the depths of the Great Ocean, her womb, Binah brought forth all things that are in manifestation. Our scientists tell us that the whole field of physical manifestation is simply a great ocean of vibrating energy whose basic form of vibration is sound.[3] It may be concluded that the individual who knows the science of making sound, which is the vehicle of thought, and correlates this articulate expression with other forms of vibration, has at his disposal a tremendous instrument to affect extraordinary and great change in his body and his environment. The initiates in the temples of Egypt were masters in the use of sound and color as instruments for raising the frequencies in the bodies of the candidates for Initiation.[4]

It is out of Sound that every form comes, in Sound every form lives, and through Sound are all changes to form affected. Man, who is the transformer of his environment, is able to effect change by his observation of nature. Then, by the reduction of his observation to words, he is able to articulate them through speech. These words he strings together in his mind as he plans the creation of new forms. All definite thought that has the power to change form is thought put into words, and thought is simply speech heard by our inner ears even when they are not vocalized. Man is, therefore, the planetary or microcosmic center of active intelligence and, therefore, the center for the perpetuation of creation in our planetary scheme.

Sound is an atmospheric vibration and when raised in vibratory rate by the continuous doubling of its pulsation will ascend to a correspondence with the electrical octaves. When these sound vibrations are registered by the sight center through the eyes, these sensations are expressed as specific colors.[5] Sound, heat, light and electricity are the manifestations of the movement of the basic elements of air, water and fire with which mankind works; sound and light are the electro-magnetic phenomena of this activity. Ageless Wisdom indicates that when we intone "words of power" we make use of the definite correlation between sound vibration and the formative forces of nature, and that every sound vibration and every intoned word of power has its own correspondence to form. Sounds and words have actual shapes and every substance in the universe is related in its basic structure to light. Colors are forces of energy and through the seven variations in the light spectrum these seven fundamental colors have definite correspondences in the human body.[6]

Each sound ray carries intelligence and is encoded with information for shape, hue and tone. The three alchemical elements of fire, air and water express themselves as Sulphur, Mercury and Salt respectively and as the three primary colors of red, yellow and blue. These three vibrations make up the soul force and are the building blocks of the creation of the vehicle of personality and all matter. It is important to note that all things in creation contain the same basic elements and are different only by the proportion and arrangements of the atoms.[7]

The Egoic or Soul triangle on the Tree of Life is comprised of the combined cosmic forces of Geburah, Chesed and Tiphareth, and the combined planetary energies and vibrations of Mars, Jupiter and Mercury.

The seven rays of energy projected from Akasha make up the triangular form of the soul and the cubical form of the body or personality vehicle. The tone and note of these three soul energies is responsible for the nature and constitution of man. Colors are spoken of as warm or cold and it is these effects, which have a definite impact on one's personal life and the consciousness of humanity.

The color Red is the first fundamental color and corresponds to the element of fire, the note C natural on the musical scale, and has the sensation of red. It is produced by the longest and slowest visible light-rays. The subtle principle of sight is assigned to this vibration whose form is triangular. Red is related to the second chakra located above the genitals in the body called the Mars center. It corresponds to the alchemical metal of iron and is identified with the prostatic plexus or the adrenal glands.

This force is very active in the motor centers of the brain and works in every voluntary and involuntary muscle to give energy, strength, courage and activity. It is active in the functioning of the reproductive organs in both men and women. Its influence is hot and dry and tends to incite one to action. This is the color of Aries and the planet Mars whose initiating quality began humanity on his adventure into form.[8] When the red vibration is well balanced in an individual, he is very self motivated and has the power to motivate others. When this vibration is unbalanced and too strong it leads to harshness, cruelty, dictatorial and animalistic behaviors. Its nature is to break down forms so as to provide the materials needed for new arrangements of forms. The red vibration corresponds to the Tower, Key 16 in Qabalistic Tarot.

The second of the basic colors is yellow and corresponds to the musical note of E, and the higher brain or cerebrum, which is its organ of expression. Its form is spherical. The quality assigned to this vibration is a pure whirling motion and the subtle principle of touch, which is said to be the primary sense from which all other senses develop.[9] The pineal gland, a reddish-white, coned shaped organ near the center of the brain, is the most important center through which the yellow vibration manifests. The other principal areas for the manifestation of yellow are the shoulders, arms, hands and lungs. These parts of the body are the primary instruments of human art and labor and the hands are the tools by which civilization, the handiwork of man, is created. The function of the lungs in controlled breathing plays an essential role in the transmutation of consciousness. This yellow vibration corresponds to the Crown chakra and to the interior star of Mercury whose alchemical metal is that of quicksilver and is the metal of the air sign Gemini, which is ruled by the planet Mercury.[10] The yellow vibration is also active in the upper part of the small intestines where the alchemical operation in the process of digestion and assimilation converts food into chyle, a substance needed for the act of transformation. Yellow is midway in the scale between the stimulating red and the depressant blue. It stimulates the higher function of the brain and is of assistance in the development of mental alertness and discrimination. It also assists in establishing emotional balance. An excess of this yellow vibration leads to indecision and a state of mental depression. Key 1, the Magician, represents this color vibration in Tarot.

The third basic color is blue and corresponds to the tone of G-sharp. The principal center of this vibration is the pituitary gland in the brain. The subtle forms taken by this vibration are crescent and triangular. It is called the Master gland and endocrinologists discovered that this organ regulates all bodily rhythms. Even the bony growth of the skeleton is among these. This gland controls the rates of respiration, periods of waking and sleeping and the cycle of menstruation. The pituitary gland is also the instrument associated with telepathy as in putting us in touch with persons at a distance much like the radio does. This center correlates, in the body, with all of the communication networks on our planet.

In addition to the regulation of the rhythms of the body, the vibrations from this center are the connective activity which links together the tiny cells from which the body is built. Every cell is in its own way a living entity and a distinct personality. The blue vibration, working through the pituitary body, is the associative and coordinating influence, which combines trillions of cell-lives into an organic whole.[11]

This blue vibration is also very active in the functioning of the stomach and the mammary glands of women. It also influences the esophagus, the thoracic duct, the upper lobes of the liver, the lower lobes of the lungs and the diaphragm. Furthermore, the blue vibration influences the function of the organs in the vicinity of the throat, the larynx, the tonsils, the palate, the lower jaw, the ears, the atlas and cervical vertebrae, the carotid artery and the jugular vein. When this blue vibration is strong and well developed, all these bodily organs are healthy. Individuals in whose lives this color is a dominant factor are sensitive, emotional, and psychic and possess a strong sense of rhythm. These persons love music, dancing and usually have great retentive memories. A deficiency in the blue vibration results in poor memory, general insensibility, a lack of rhythm and a harsh temper. When this vibration is defective a lack of co-ordination results throughout the community of cell-lives and this, in addition to other things, sets up a pre-disposition to cancer and other abnormal growths.

The chakra corresponding to the blue vibration is the Moon center or Ajna Chakra. It is located between the eyebrows and is represented by the High Priestess in Qabalistic Tarot. Though the color vibration of this chakra is blue, the Yogis of the East declare it to be "white as the Moon". The alchemical metal associated with this center is silver.

These three vibrations of Red, Yellow and Blue form what is called the plane of higher mind or the Higher Mental Plane. The cycle of each individual in incarnation is colored by the level of intensity and frequency of his soul force; and what is needed to condition the personality vehicle for the next rung of his evolutionary spiral and the role the individual is to play in a particular world cycle.

In another step-down process, the soul, using a mixture of these three primary colors, produces the next three hues and vibrations in matter, which form the astral vehicle or Chariot of the incarnated man, in which the Soul carries out the divine plan in form. The fundamental but secondary colors of green, orange and violet make up the triangle of the animal soul on the astral plane and finally, the kingdom of flesh in the physical plane we know as the body. This body is the recipient of all the vibrations flowing down from above and known to us as fire, air, water and earth. It is from this Astral Light or Ether of the astral triangle, which we also call the fifth element that these four elements came. On the Tree of Life, this is the sphere of Yesod.[12]

In descending order, the desire body manifests first as the element of air, which is said to have a predominant color of blue with a yellow-green tinge but manifesting mostly as green. This element refers to the seventh sphere on the Tree of Life, Netzach or the desire body. The green vibration corresponds to the note of F-sharp on the musical scale and its principal physiological center is in the throat, particularly the thyroid and parathyroid glands. It is in the throat area that strong emotions are felt. This vibration greatly affects the kidneys and the lumbar region of the spine and also influences the skin and the sense of touch.

When this vibration is functioning well, it makes for grace and symmetry in physical action and form. This green vibration also enhances artistic abilities and stimulates creative imagination.[13] The individuals for whom this vibration is well balanced have good taste, love beauty and are fond of pleasure and the simple pleasures of life. When this vibration is weak, the mental and emotional centers in the body are weakened. When there is an excess of this vibration in the body, the individual suffers from emotional over-indulgence, is sensation seeking and wastes much time in mere enjoyment. The chakra in the body to which this vibration corresponds is the throat or Venus center represented in Tarot by the Empress, Key 3. The alchemical metal associated with this vibration and chakra is copper, which is the metal of Venus.

The element of fire corresponds to the eighth sphere. It refers to the intellect, which in turn is symbolized by the sphere of Hod on the Tree of Life. Its color manifestation is that of orange, which is a combination of yellow, and red. It corresponds to the tone of D-natural and has the quality of being hot and dry but not as intense as the red vibration. When it is well developed in the body it expresses itself as strength, health and vitality. When these attributes find expression in the individual's consciousness, one is frank, magnanimous, generous, humane, as well as having a firm and honorable disposition. When, however, when there is a vibrational obstruction in the body, the above-mentioned temperaments are reversed and the opposite qualities become manifested. An overabundance of the orange vibration in the body can be seen as domineering, over ambitious, exhibitionist and very wasteful of vitality and other resources.

In the sympathetic nervous system, this vibration manifests itself through the cardiac ganglion, which is a center above and behind the heart and governs the function of the heart. It is through this center that the cosmic life-energy enters the personal field. It can be compared to the main switch through which electricity is transmitted from the electrical gauge box outside a building to the interior. The chakra corresponding to this vibration is the Heart, which is said to be the dwelling place of the Most High; as well as being the place where the uncaused sound or the Voice of the silence can be heard. In alchemy the heart center is the interior star called the Sun, which corresponds to alchemical gold; and also to the Sun, Key 19, in Tarot.[14]

The alchemical water follows next. Its predominant color is white with violet as its secondary color. Ageless Wisdom states that when the colors of red, blue and yellow, the three primary colors, are in perfect balance, the color white is produced. Yesod, the element of water is the sphere of the Moon called Foundation and this is the foundation on which Man is established. The color of Yesod is essentially the same as Kether, which is white. Yesod is the reflection of the one Self, seated in Kether, which is called the Ether of the Wise. It is the reproductive center from which physical manifestation proceeded. It is from this center in Kether that the whole Tree of Life with its twenty-two paths and ten Sephiroth came into manifestation by means of mental activity. Yesod is the seat of the vital or animal soul. It is also the center of the lower man. The color manifested by Yesod in this cycle is violet, which is a mixture of red and blue and will influence the process of synthesis, which is the dominant activity of the Aquarian Age. When red, the primal fire of thought in the head is merged with blue the water of emotions in the heart, under the influence of the yellow of air in mind, we will create the color white or absolute unity. This is the goal of this Age. Then we will have created heaven on Earth.

Violet corresponds to the tone of A-sharp or B-flat on the musical scale. The main center of the violet vibration is the solar plexus or epigastric ganglion. It is also called the abdominal brain. It controls the functioning of the stomach and the entire sympathetic nervous system. The Ancients believed that the entire record of the story of man's involution and evolution, from the beginning of this cycle to the present is recorded here.[15] The other areas affected by this vibration are the coccygeal and sacral regions of the spine, the iliac arteries and veins, the sciatic nerves, the femur, the hips and the thighs. The feet and toes are also an area in which the violet vibration dominates. The pituitary gland and the solar plexus work closely together and their combined effects influence the activities in the stomach, liver and mammary glands. When this vibration is in normal flow, there is a fondness for outdoor activity simply because all the bodily functions are basically sound. Its manifestation in the individual expresses psychologically as a love for ceremony, good manners, charity, interest in established forms of religion, respect for law and order as well as a balanced conservative attitude toward life in general.

The individual in whom this vibration is weak displays the opposite of the above-mentioned mental qualities and suffers from poor circulation. When this vibration is too strong, the individual can be seen as pompous, materialistic, rigidly conservative and overly conventional. The chakra to which the violet vibration corresponds is the interior star of Jupiter or the Solar Plexus chakra represented by the Wheel of Fortune, Key 10.

The sphere of Malkuth or the Kingdom on the Tree of Life exists in the Physical Plane as the Body and represents alchemical earth whose form is cubical. The color representing this sphere is blue-violet or indigo in the cosmic man. The principal center in the body for this vibration is the nervous system and the sacral plexus near the base of the spine. The function of this center in the body is to excrete waste. It also influences the functions involving the transmission of life from one generation to another. This vibration also influences the skin, the sweat glands, the knees, the ankles, the kidneys and the lumbar region of the spine, as well as the vasomotor system and the bones.

This center at the base of the spine is what the Eastern philosophers call the place of the Kundalini or the coiled-up serpent. It is like a storage battery, which is charged with the residual energy left over from our many bodily functions. The blue-violet vibration in us is that which limits and restricts us for our own good. Individuals in whom this vibration is in normal flow operate with poise, deliberation, and total concentration.[16] However, an overactive manifestation of these vibrations results in fear and in a poisoning of the body through the retention of both mental and physical waste. On the other hand a deficiency leads to dreaming without action, eccentricity and rashness.

This blue-violet vibration in the body corresponds to the Root Chakra at the base of the spine and to the World, Key 21, in the Tarot.

Out of this mixing bowl of Akasha centered in Yesod, which is also the reproductive center and house to the etheric envelop, intelligence shaped and fashioned animal-man and then divine man. In geometric representation he is symbolized by a square on which the divine triangle sits; for this reason the ancients used the pyramid and the pentagram to symbolize MAN.

When Man and the Physical plane are balanced and equilibrated it will assume the same triangular form and reflect the others on the planes above on the Tree of Life. Then Mankind will be illumed and the Earth will become a sacred planet.[17]

Light, says Eliphas Levi, is the efficient agent of form and life for it is both movement and heat and when it succeeds in fixing itself, in order to be polarized round a center, it produces a living being. It then attracts whatever plastic or flexible substance is necessary in order to perfect and preserve it. The Bible rightly calls this substance, which is formed of earth and water in the final analysis, the 'clay of the earth'. Light is an instrument of Spirit and is the primary physical manifestation of divine breath, which is created by God eternally. Man, in the image of God, modifies it and then multiplies it.[18]

Breath is pure Spirit and Breath is Life and it is through this primal spiritual energy, which we call Prana, and is concentrated in the earth's atmosphere, that all things come into being. It is this vital substance that subsists in the air that we breathe and it is under the power of breath as well as under the controlled and directed focus of the mind that transformation in man from ordinary (Man) to God-Man is accomplished. Prana is said to have two qualities: one hot and fiery as in the Sun and the other moist and cool as in the Moon.

These seven vibrations of sound and color expressed themselves first as three and then four. With their attendant complexion and type they emerged as four great divisions of the present human race. As consciousness progressed, each race emerged in ordered progression carrying the divine idea or coded information in light and color for the expression of a certain quality and shape in each cycle.

H.P Blavatsky in the Secret Doctrine tells us that on the evolutionary pathway the first form-like substance in manifestation was moon-colored-white. What followed next in the transformation process was the red man. In the third transformation man was yellow and in the fourth he was blue-black or indigo.

The first race was said to have neither type nor color and was hardly an objective form even though it was colossal. Mankind was then expressed in three great divisions namely, red-yellow, blue-black and brown-white. The three fundamental elements in the composition of human organism are fire, water and air and they express themselves to the human sight as red, blue and yellow respectively. When mixed in variable qualities and quantities with the white tissues they give rise to the numerous shades seen in the human family.

The Aryan race, which is the Fifth Root Race, includes all of humanity as well as including all the color vibrations which vary from dark brown, blue-black, red-brown-yellow down to the whitest creamy color. They are all of the One and from the same stock - from one single progenitor.[19]

Blavatsky further states that light yellow is the color of the first SOLID human race, which appeared after the middle of the Third Root race in Lemuria. At this period in human evolution the development of the mental envelop and the emergence of intelligence took place. Furthermore, it was at this time that the inversion of the mental fire into matter, which is now expressed as materiality became apparent. This process transformed the remnant of Humanity which became "black with sin" into the red-yellow races from which the red Indians and the Mongolians are descendants. Finally, we have the brown-white races that now, together with the yellow races, form the bulk of humanity.[20]

The ancients have used the Pentagram for eons to represent MAN. The head is the apex and the two out-stretched arms and legs represent the four arms of the pentagram. Similarly the capstone, with its four sides and corners of the base of the Great Pyramid, is a representation of Man.

This symbol is the Quintessence clothed in Divine Light called flesh. Qabalah also assigns to this symbol the names of Shin, Yod, Heh, Vav and Heh, which are Astral Light or Ether, fire, earth, air and water. These are the names of God and are also attributed to Man. The Great Pyramid has been likened to the universe, and the capstone, to Man. As Spirit is the capstone of the mind so is God the epitome of the whole. Man has been likened to a rough unfinished block taken from the quarry and, by the secret culture of the mysteries, he is gradually being transformed into a trued and perfected pyramidal capstone. He, the temple, is only complete when the initiate himself becomes the living apex through which the divine power is focused into the diverging structure below.[21]

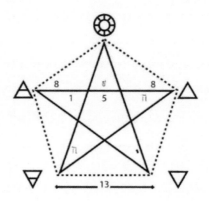

The Pentagram, God housed in form

In sacred geometry and esoteric numerology, the pentagram reveals the nature of God in form. When the pentagram is enclosed or clothed to form a pentagon, we have a five equal-sided figure, to which occultists have assigned 13 units to each side, making the perimeter of the pentagon the number 65 when added together. This is the number Qabalists assign to the Lord or Adonai. The length of each line of the pentagram is assigned 21 units, which is the number of the Divine name given to Eheyeh and Kether. The number twenty-one and the number, three, when reduced, is the number of the One Life seated at the heart of Man. This force is none other than the Creative Principle or divine mother seated at the heart of all life. This force is projected out into the six directions of space: above, east, west, north, south and below to created the manifested world. The Cube formed by these six directions has come to symbolize Man and the Universe. The total length of the lines when totaled gives us the number 105; when reduced the number is six, which relates to Tiphareth, the sixth emanation on the Tree of Life, and is the representation of conscious and regenerated Man. The works of man, symbolized by the Pentagram, are both circumscribed and conditioned by the Being of the Lord. They are also special manifestations of the spiritual power proceeding from the divine light in Kether. The pentagram is a symbol of the expression of the relationship of God to man and of man to nature. It is a powerful affirmation of the truth that whatever is done by man is actually a final link in a series of activities which were begun by God. By and through man, the splendor and the Beauty of the Divine can be expressed and experienced with all of his senses.[22]

In occultism the number 65 also represents the summation of the Great Work. This number five is the five-pointed star and is the sign of the Christos. It represents the I Am presence in the heart of man, as well as, the number six or the hexagram, which is the six-pointed star and together they are the symbols of the cosmic forces surrounding man and constituting his environment. The pentagram is the sign of the mind as having dominion over the forces of nature while at the same time the hexagram represents the cosmic forces and laws, which make up the whole field of activity revolving around the central I AM.

The number 65 also means temple or palace with direct reference to the "Palace of Holiness" in the midst of which is the sanctum sanctorum. It is in this place in Solomon's temple, which sits the Ark of the Covenant, and is the site of the Radiant Presence of God. This temple is Man who is also the temple-not- made-with-hands in which the power now dwells that made the worlds, and who rules everything in the universe. It is here that Tiphareth, the regenerated Man who is named Adam Kadmon, rules in the Kingdom of Malkuth as the King. He rules with wisdom and power due to the consciousness he has evolved; he now understands his kinship with the Divine Source as the Son of God. This idea is stated by the Rosicrucian aphorism: "Man is the Son of God, and there is no God but Man". He is the Prodigal

Son returned from his journey in the far country with the Wisdom, Knowledge and Understanding by which s/he is elevated to the status of a wise ruler who is symbolically Solomon.

Manly P Hall, in The Symbolism of the Human Body, states that the human body has been known by the ancients as one of the most universal of all symbols. The mysteries of every culture teach that the laws, elements and powers of the universe are epitomized in the human constitution. Everything that exists outside of man has an analogue within man. The universe in its immensity is immeasurable, profoundly inconceivable and beyond that which the mortal mind is able to grasp. When man is temporarily permeated with divine enthusiasm it becomes possible for him to have only a partial comprehension of this immensity. Only then is he able to perceive in part the celestial glory in which all creation basks.[23]

Man is incapable of imprinting upon his rational soul a perfect image of the multiform expression of celestial activity even in periods of his greatest illumination. So, realizing the futility of attempting to cope intellectually with that which transcends the comprehension of the rational faculties, the early philosophers turned their attention from the inconceivable divinity to the more tangible body of man or himself, for within the nature of man is manifested all the mysteries of the external spheres.

The philosophers of antiquity came to regard the greater universe as the Macrocosm and the Divine Life controlling its functions as the Macroprosophus. Man, the microcosm, is controlled and supported by the microprosophus. The analogies between the organs and functions of the microcosmic man and the Macrocosmic Man have been the subject of investigation and the object of learning for initiates throughout past millennia.[24]

From the earliest times the human figure has symbolized the divine power in all its intricate manifestations. The priests of antiquity accepted man as their textbook and through the study of him they learned to understand the greater and more hidden mysteries of the celestial plan of which they were a part.

Based on the assumption that man is actually fashioned in the image of God, the initiated minds of the past ages built the great structure of theology upon the foundation of the human body. It is little known to the religious world that the science of biology is the foundation on which its doctrines and principles are based. Modern men of divinity believe that many of the codes and laws are direct revelations to them from the divine. In reality, they are the fruitage of ages of patient delving into the intricacies of the human constitution. This is how these infinite wonders were revealed to them by such study.

An anatomical analogy can be traced to the creation myths in all sacred books of the world. A familiarity with embryology and obstetrics will reveal the basis of the allegory concerning Adam and Eve and the Garden of Eden. The nine degrees of the Eleusinian Mysteries, the Brahmanic legend of Vishnu's incarnations, the story of the Universal Egg, the Scandinavian myth of Ginnungagap (the cleft in space in which the seed of the world is sown), and the use of the fish as the symbol of the paternal generative power, are all indications or evidence that the origin of theological speculations are based upon the biological functions of the human body.[25]

The philosophers of old realized that man was himself the Key to the riddle of Life because he is the living image of the Divine Plan. In this Age and those to come, humanity will come to realize more fully the solemn import of the ancients' words, "The proper study of mankind is man".

Both God and Man have a twofold constitution of which the superior part is invisible and the inferior part is visible and in both there is an intermediary sphere. This is the point where the invisible and the visible spheres meet. The spiritual nature of God controls His objective universal form, which is in fact a crystallized idea. The spiritual nature of man, which is the invisible cause and controlling power of his visible material personality and the kingdoms below him, likewise, controls his planetary form. It concludes, therefore, that the spirit of man bears the same relationship to his material body that God bears to the objective universe.

The sacred mysteries taught that spirit or life was before form and that what comes before includes all that is after it, and since Spirit came before form, form is included within the realm of Spirit. It is also a popular belief that man's Spirit is within his body. However, according to the conclusions of philosophy and theology, Spirit first circumscribes an area and then manifests within it. From a philosophical perspective, form, being a part of Spirit, is within spirit but Spirit is more than the sum of form. So, as the material nature of man is within the sum of Spirit, so is the Universal Nature, including the sidereal system, within the all-pervading essence of God, the Universal Spirit.[26]

Ancient wisdom also holds that all bodies, spiritual or material, have three bodies, which are called by some: an upper, middle and a lower, with the middle being the link. The three universal centers are represented by the three suns or three aspects of the sun; they are, the Sun or Light in its abstract or absolute form, which is unrevealed and is called darkness; the Light manifested or proceeding from the sun's source, and the sun or Light reflected in its splendor as it is communicated in nature.

It is in the human body that the heart, which is in the midst of the physical being, becomes the superior center from which Spirit manifests. The Heart is known by occultists to be the most spiritual and mysterious organ in the body. This being so, the brain then becomes, the second center and the link between the superior and inferior worlds or that, which existed before and after, and is accorded the greatest physical dignity. The third or lower center is assigned the position of least physical dignity but the greatest physical importance, that of the reproductive system.

The Heart is symbolically the source of life and the brain is the link between which rational intelligence, life and form are united. The reproductive system is the source of that power by which the physical universe is produced. The ideals and aspirations of the individual are also conditioned by which one of these three centers of power dominates in his life expression. In the materialist, his lower center is the strongest, in the intellectual, the higher center or brain is strongest, but in the Initiate, the middle center or Heart is strongest because he has gained mastery on all levels and now bathes the two extremes in a flood of spiritual glory. He controls in a wholesome fashion both the mind and the body.[27]

The three degrees of initiation into the Ancient Mysteries were all given in chambers representing the three centers of the Universal bodies and if possible the temple was constructed in the form of the human body. The candidate would pass between the feet of understanding and receive the highest degree in the point corresponding to the brain. The first degree then, was the material mystery and its symbol was the reproductive system. It raised the candidate through various degrees of concrete thought. The second degree was given in the chamber corresponding to the heart but represented the middle power, which was the mental link. Here the candidate was initiated into the mysteries of abstract thought and was lifted as high as his mind was capable of penetrating. He then passed into the chamber that was analogous to the brain and through this center, occupied the highest position in the temple. It is analogous to the heart and is of the greatest dignity. In the brain chamber, the heart mystery is given. Here, for the first time the initiate truly comprehends the immortal words which are: "*As a man thinketh in his heart, so is he.*"

There are seven hearts in the brain and so are there seven brains in the heart. This is, however, a matter of super-physics and is now becoming more apparent as more disciples take the major initiations.[28] When man penetrates into himself and more profoundly into the knowledge of himself, he finds in himself both intellect and the order of things. However, when he proceeds into his interior, into the adytum or inner temple of his soul, he perceives, with his eyes closed, which is without the aid of the lower mind, the genus of the gods and the unity of beings. All things are in man physically and through this, man is capable of knowing all things through igniting the powers and the images of wholes that he contains within him. The body of man should, therefore, not be considered as the individual but only as the house of the individual, in the same way that the temple is the House of God. In a state of grossness or perversion, man's body has become the tomb or prison of a divine principle. When the individual is in a state of unfoldment or regeneration, his body is the House or Abode of the Divine by whose creative powers it was fashioned.

Man is essentially a permanent and immortal principle and only his bodies pass through cycles of birth and death. During each cycle of birth in the earth-life reality, the immortal man that he is dwells in a body or house of unreality until s/he is temporarily liberated from it through death or permanently through illumination.[29] As an immortal principle, man's body becomes the vehicle through which the whole universe evolves. The four elements, the planets, the twelve signs of the zodiac, and the constellations all have their analogues in the human body. The hidden God within mankind's body is said to dwell in the marrow of the bones.

Thus is created the Grand Man, which is called the Adam Kadmon or God in form. He is the sum total of all things and is at the Center of all Life. He is the creator and the created. No being can become God unless he passes through the human cycles and so happy are those who are born. Man, He is the Great Mystery. It is for Himself that he has searched all creation to find!

Chapter Seven

The Seven Stages of Spiritual Unfoldment

Solomon's Seal: The merge of matter and spirit and all the opposites

The Grand Cycle of the next twenty-five thousand years will be the overarching influence under which mankind will continue to evolve. In addition, the next twenty-one hundred years, the Age of Aquarius, will have an enormous impact on humanity's return to the Father's House. This great in-breath is the inward spiraling movement of the Primal Fire and Water that provides the optimum conditions and will result in humanity remembering who he is, and superseding his original state.

The seven stages of spiritual return begin with the Fool, Key 0 who represents the planet Uranus and the ruler of the Age of Aquarius.

It represents Absolute Unity and it is this Joker who will provide the beacon through which the Star Sirius will lead humanity Home.

Key 0: The Fool

The Father is waiting earnestly to welcome you home and when you return he will celebrate your return with great ceremony, and elevate you to a position beyond that which you held and also beyond your wildest imagination.

Key Zero is the symbol of the Cause of all Causes, the Limitless Light, the Source of All that is. It is the egg out of which all things in manifestation are issued and it is into this Source that all things must return. This is the place from which the Prodigal Son started out on his journey eons ago. He has experienced the extremes of physical, emotional and mental life and now he must synthesize these experiences. He must gain the deep understanding of the nature of his experiences as both the traveler and the traveled to comprehend or master the reason for his journey.[1]

The finite mind cannot comprehend the infinite and only through experiences can the infinite reveal itself to the individual, through the registering of its secret nature on the soul of the traveler. The traveler must be a conscious traveler, being observant not to miss any important detail while on the journey, for the Path of Return is one of remembering.

The journey of the Prodigal Son coming home is also that of Planet Earth on its way to becoming a sacred planet. The reason for the traveler's descent into the depth of matter was to carry with him the divine idea, to experience and then to consciously recollect. This is what the paths of involution and now evolution are about. The process of recollection must relate the principles of above to the experiences of below, the without to the within, in order to extrapolate an accurate and meaningful understanding of the experiences.[2]

The seven stages of enlightenment involve seven principles. These principles are universal, impartial and impersonal. They apply to everyone and everything in nature, to the poor and to the rich. They are at work in all the spheres of human living whether the individual is aware of them or not. In order to get back home one must consciously apply these principles to his or her life. These principles were given to us by our elder brothers and sisters who have figured them out in their struggle out of form, and in their love and compassion for those coming behind, they have left them for us as a guide.[3] They know the way because they traveled it and arrived back home safely. It makes sense therefore, that instead of re-inventing the wheel we would look at the map and chart out our individual course. Some people have decided to take the scenic route but one must always remember that there is a timetable for Planet Earth and also for our individual end game. However, the journey can be continued on another planet for those who get lost and become over-identified with the scenery! There are others who don't know the way to get home but are sure that the route left for us by our experienced brothers and sisters isn't the right one - the ego plays many tricks on us. We have to watch out for that old serpent. S/he is a trickster and will play any game with us we want to play!

Again, at each stage, we will examine the principles involved, the medium through which that principle operates and then the manifested stage of unfoldment. We will be using the twenty-two Keys of the Qabalistic Tarot to help us on this journey.

The Keys we are using might be off-putting to many who have pre-conceived ideas about the Tarot as being playing cards and unholy and cannot imagine how these cards could possibly have any effect in one's enlightenment. There is an old maxim that says, nothing is ever what it appears to be; it would be good to remember this always on this journey, as this information will come in very handy. You should remember that this journey is an occult journey and may be different from anything you have embarked on before. Occult by definition means secret or hidden. The reason this knowledge appears to be hidden is because the majority of humanity was not ready to see and, therefore, not able to comprehend it. One cannot see until he has given himself permission to see and one will not give himself permission to see until he has made himself ready to see. Sight is a very important aspect on this journey and, in fact, it is an important component of the first stage or stop on this journey. Remember this path is not for the faint-hearted but for the mature aspirant who is ready to take his next step up the ladder and is seeking for the opportunity to move forward. Lucifer, the Star of the Morning, leads the way into matter in order to begin a great adventure, an adventure that will aid in the discovery of our deepest potentials as gods on Earth.[4]

This occult journey requires that we take off the blinders and allow ourselves to see what we might not have wanted to see and to own what is usually projected onto someone or something else. An occultist is a mature human on his way to unfolding the God-man. He takes full responsibility for who he is by having full knowledge of whom he is.

Each stage of unfoldment involves three Keys. The first represents a principle. The second, an agency through which that principle works and third, the manifestation of that principle called a stage of unfoldment; the Chinese remind us that a picture is worth a thousand words. These Qabalistic Tarot picture books were left for us in symbolic form by the sages of old who met in the great city of Fez, Morocco when persecution of religious freedom was at its zenith.

Key 1: The Magician   *Key 8: Strength*   *Key 15: The Devil*

The first stage of unfoldment involves Keys One, Eight and Fifteen. The Magician or Key One is the principle guiding the first stage of unfoldment. The Magician is a representation of Mercury or Hermes the messenger of the gods, the transmitter of wisdom and knowledge and it is the self-conscious aspect of man. It is the initiating, creative aspect, capable of formulating premises and seed-ideas. It is the interpreter of the Divine Idea or Will to be manifested in form and becomes the transformer of the personality. This divine knowledge and wisdom engages the mind in the formulation of premises for the control of the forces acting below the surface. The application of these divine laws allows the aspirant to experience success, health and long life. The misunderstanding and improper application of these laws has been responsible for the pain, suffering and death mankind has experienced. The same laws that have been applied toward misery, if applied correctly, will achieve liberation. Self-consciousness is a function of the human kingdom only. It is man and his ability for conscious thought that must aid nature in its further evolution beyond the human kingdom and in achieving the full flowering of self-consciousness.[5] Nature unaided always fails because the human factor is needed to bring about the perfection of the powers that are only partially expressed in the kingdoms below man. This expression of the Primal Will through man makes him more aware of his environment and thus he becomes a better instrument for the expression of his true Self.[6]

The agent used by self-consciousness to carry out the Will of Super-consciousness is the coiled-up serpent power or Kundalini energy at the base of the spine. This energy is symbolized in the Qabalistic Tarot as Key 8 and is called Strength. The letter "S" is a diagrammatic representation of the path of the "serpent power" as it moves through the nervous system of man. It is the force responsible for the strength and tonicity of the muscles and for strength of will and mind. Key 8 represents the zodiacal sign of Leo with the Lion as its animal symbol. The secret to the use of this sexual force is that its essential nature is the exhaustible energy of the One Spirit. This Magical Agent is used by everyone, everyday and is the cosmic electricity and Universal life-principle. It is the force that takes form in everything in existence and builds them from within. It is essential, therefore, that whatever one chooses to create must be initiated with clarity, specificity and purpose in order to bring about the intended result.[7] The woman in this Key is a symbol for the human kingdom and is the controller of all the forces below the human level. She has yellow hair, which signifies her evolved state of consciousness.

She wears a crown of flowers, a reference to the Primal Will or Kether and her rulership of the organic process of nature. Flowers are the reproductive organs of the vegetable kingdom of which the rose is the highest expression. Red roses are a symbol of active desires to be later transmuted into the white rose during the process of evolution. The garland of roses around her waist and the lion's neck makes the figure eight, indicating a series of desires woven together. When these desires are brought into harmony with the laws of nature, mankind can achieve true dominion over the kingdoms of nature. Her white dress indicates divine unity and the purified aspect of sub-consciousness, as well as the fact that intelligent application of self-consciousness leads to the personal realization that ALL is ONE. She tames the Red Lion, symbolic of the animal nature in man, by the development of the higher mind and right thinking. The Lion, King of the Jungle, represents rulership, courage, tenacity, resolve, will and decision. This conscious intelligence in man makes him able to bring under his control the creative forces within him, below him and around him for the manifestation of the divine will in form. All the kingdoms are represented here: the mountain, the roses, the lion and the human are all the highest levels of expression of the mineral, vegetable, animal and human kingdoms respectively. All of the cells in the human body are a "little" animal and are waiting for the conscious direction of the evolved human mind. The Path of Adeptship requires knowledge of this Great Magical Agent, the serpent, the deceiver and the concealer of the true nature of things. The Adept, however, looks beneath the surface of what the world reports by using the five senses. He detects the hidden relationships by putting his mind and emotions under the guidance of the inner Teacher, the Hierophant, so that he can be properly taught.

The first stage of unfoldment is also symbolized by Key 15, the Devil, and is called Renewal. The Devil is the symbol for Archangel Uriel of the direction north and represents the sign of Capricorn, which is ruled by the planet Saturn, with the planet Mars exalted in this sign. Lead is the metal associated with the planet Saturn and must be transmuted into gold on the path of evolution. The Hebrew word for Key 15 is "Ayin" and directly relates to the "All-seeing Eye of God". It is this Devil that goads mankind on to liberation and is, therefore, his Redeemer when he removes the mask by allowing himself to see.

We are told that the solution to any problem lies in the problem itself. We will, therefore, examine all the symbolisms of this Key in order to gain a clearer understanding of the nature of the bondage in which mankind is entangled so that he can see how to liberate himself.

This image on Key 15 is one of the most feared and misunderstood in all cultures everywhere. It is also one of the most powerful and important Keys of the twenty-two secret paths of wisdom. The understanding of this Key is, therefore, essential to one's freedom because anything we fear owns us. The image of the Devil presented to us in this picture by the Masters of Wisdom can easily be termed an absurdity and is responsible for the atrocities of human behavior due to misinterpretation. The image is that of an androgyne goat with the wings of a bat, the arms and hands of a man, and the legs and feet of an eagle.

His wings refer to the Devil being "the prince of the power of the air". Its legs and feet are that of the eagle, the symbol of Scorpio, a fixed water sign that rules the reproductive system. Unless this Scorpio force in man is purified in the fires of tests and trials, he remains in bondage. His uplifted hand gives a gesture quite different from that of the Magician, which indicates the transmission of a focused stream of energy. Instead, his gesture is that of the uplifted hand and open palm, the dissipation of forces, displaying the Saturnine symbol of limitation. The position of the fingers are in contrast to the esoteric gesture of the Hierophant and so the Devil seems to be saying that whatever is visible and can be grasped by the five senses is all there is. This is one of the greatest fallacies and is responsible for the hold that materialism has on humanity and the bondage of his existence. The red eyes of the Devil's correspond to the red planet Mars, which is exalted in the sign of Capricorn and is also the ruler of Aries. The function of sight and the destructive action of Mars go hand in hand. Mars destroys the erroneous perceptions of reality so that we can see into the true reality beyond appearances.

Below the Devil's navel is the sign of Mercury and refers to the Virgo center in the body, the small intestines, and is the place where the alchemical process of digestion and assimilation takes place. The lower half of the symbol is red indicating that the combined action of the mind and the bodily responses represented by the red cross are responsible for the transformative process of food which produces "chyle" or liquid gold and releases it into the bloodstream. The inverted torch in the Devil's left hand gives little light and is indicative of the limited light that results from misinterpretation of experiences. The inverted pentagram between the Devil's two horns is one of the most evil of all the signs in black magic. The real essence of black magic is mental inversion that is rooted in the idea that the true Self of man, symbolized by the apex of the pentagram, is dominated by the four elements composing his physical environment. The inverted pentagram is, therefore, a false notion since it can never be true that the matter, which it created, can dominate Spirit.

The Devil sits on a half-cube representing the imperfect understanding of the physical world whose true representation is a cube. On the front of this half-cube is a ring to which two smaller human-like figures are fastened by chains, one male the other female, with direct references to the self-conscious and subconscious minds of man. The bondage of illusion symbolized here is a result of mankind's erroneous interpretation of the nature of the physical universe. The hoofs, horns and tails of these prisoners demonstrate how delusion bestializes man. On careful examination, it can be seen that the chains around the necks of the man and the woman are loose enough to be removed by them at any time. However, because of the false perception they hold about their own nature, power and ability, they feel helpless and at the mercy of their circumstances.

It is of utmost importance that the aspirant understands that s/he is responsible for his own liberation, like the prodigal son who came to himself in the transformative impulse of Scorpio. When the life force or sexual energy is turned upward in the body, instead of going out, he turns around and begins to make his way home through the "stations of the cross" called the chakras.

When mankind does not understand the laws of the life-power's self-expression, the laws appear adversarial. Problems arise when we try to separate the appearance from the "Appearer". The two are one and not in opposition to each other. In the West, man seems to accept the objective world as the only reality and the East tends to interpret the objective world as being an unreal optical illusion. Ageless

Wisdom reconciles these two opposing interpretations and asserts that reality applies to both worlds. The outer world may be Maya in one sense, but what we call "matter" is really the "appearance" of what we call spirit as it enters the world of name and form, and so both are real.

The Devil is God as He is misunderstood by the unenlightened. Key 15 is a symbol of man's ignorant notions of the true nature of Reality and more importantly man's false opinions concerning his own place in the scheme of things. This ignorance is the real devil and because this ignorance can be overcome, they who set their feet upon the Way of Liberation learn to banish the devil and destroy his works. The secret for the release of mankind is to re-position the Pentagram right side up. This will occur in this New Age of Aquarius.[8]

Key 2: The High Priestess   *Key 9: The Hermit*   *Key 16: The Tower*

The second stage is that of awakening, influenced by the principle of association, symbolized by the High Priestess who is also known as the chief feminine Elder. The medium through which this principle operates is the Hermit. The High Priestess is the record keeper and memory of the universe and the individual aspirant. To her, Qabalah attributes the mode of consciousness called "The Uniting Intelligence."

She is universal subconsciousness and responds to the focused attention given by the self-consciousness for recall. She develops these seed ideas given to her by using her perfect powers of deductive reasoning. She has perfect memory of all the activity of physical matter since it was she who brought all matter into physical manifestation, not just on this planet but throughout the universe. She represents the element of water, the root matter, from which all things issued. She holds the scroll, which contains the memory of all life since the beginning of time. It is at this time in the history of humanity that this female Elder will open the book spoken of in the Book of Revelations. When the pages are read, mankind will remember his original home.

As the seat of memory, she "carries the load" of mankind's personal experiences because subconsciousness is a universal phase of the life-power's activity. Our "personal" subconsciousness is a particular manifestation of this great and all-inclusive universal subconsciousness. When women can remember who they are and what their role is in the cosmic order, balance and equality will be restored. When both men and women of all races everywhere learn how to gain access to the records of all experiences by tapping into the cosmic subconscious memories, it will be possible for us all to arrive at an accurate reconstruction of the past. Through the principle of association, symbolized by the two pillars in this Key, one black and the other white, the wider expanses of all associated ideas, thoughts and feelings are unified.[9] The seven laws of association used by the High Priestess in recall are:

1. The Law of Mentalism, which states that the totality of the universe is mental.

2. The Law of Correspondence, which can be summed up by the maxim: "All things are of the One and from the One.

3. The Law of Vibration.

4. The Law of Polarity.

5. The Law of Rhythm.

6. The Law of Cause and Effect.

7. The Law of Gender.[10]

It is through the agency of the knowledge and wisdom of the Hermit who is the symbol of Hermes, that every adept reaches enlightenment on the mountaintop of spiritual attainment. He is the Fool in his aspect of all-embracing experience. He is the wise man because age and youth are all appearances of the No-Thing. He shines the light of his knowledge, love and compassion, which is symbolized by the discriminative light of the six-pointed star coming from his lantern for all who must climb the mountain of spiritual attainment on the Path of Return. He is the loving guide who helps humanity remember his true order in the kingdom of nature.

His cap is blue, the symbol of water and of the High Priestess, which is in the shape of the Hebrew letter Yod, the Divine Fire. It is his memory of who he is, who he has been, and who he will always be that has brought him to this place of identification with the One Identity. He has shed the mask of the personality and knows his own true identity. The Hermit represents the sign of Virgo as it is ruled by Mercury, as well as being the sign in which Mercury is exalted. As stated earlier, the Virgo region of the body is the small intestines and is essential to illumination. Under the right self-conscious direction, the finer forces present in the oily, milky substance called chyle are liberated into the blood stream. It is this substance that energizes the brain centers, which assist in the experience called illumination through which one gives birth to the Christ consciousness. It is very important to understand that the process of spiritual enlightenment is a direct outcome of our physical, emotional and mental food and that the process of illumination is, in part, a physical one. This is the process that establishes the kingdom of God in the physical form and on Earth. Therefore, through right recollection represented by the High Priestess, mankind comes to know the One Identity, the Hermit, and this knowledge overthrows all structures relating to the delusion of separateness.

The Light coming from the Hermit's lantern is an aspect of the Life-Power. It is the same lightening bolt, which strikes and "knocks off" the Crown on the Tower. The lightning indicates the sudden illumination, which comes to the aspirant when he faces a particular problem boldly and has concentrated his focused and prolonged attention with the full force of the Life-Power as symbolized by the Magician, Key One. At this point, the aspirant has awakened from his dream of sense and his nightmare of bondage, and is now able to see. And so now he must act![11]

The Tower is the symbol for Key 16. It is the second stage of unfoldment and is represented by Mars, the planet of action and constructive destruction. We will now examine the symbolism for an understanding of the tower of man's imprisonment. The background, against which the Tower stands, as with the Devil, is black and is a reference to ignorance. The Tower is made of twenty-two courses of masonry and is symbolic of the twenty-two letters of the Hebrew alphabet. However, the material used in the construction of this tower is not "stone" which is the material of the wise. Instead, this structure is made of the false material "brick" which can never withstand the force of divine power and truth. The Tower is also a symbol of the structure of human speech both spoken and written, which mankind has used to imprison, isolate and suppress himself and his fellowman. The Tower is also a symbolic reference to physical human personalities, which are the structures that incorporate our false notions while at the same time they are the temples of God in which the spark of the divine resides.

The lightning flash of true perception always makes itself felt in the physical body because the body must be re-adjusted before it can be a suitable vehicle for the expression of the higher levels of consciousness. The Crown, a symbol of Will Power, is knocked off. This, however, is a false crown and embodies the false idea about will-power and the notion that every person has a will of his own, separate from the will of other persons and the Cosmic Will, the ruling power in the universe. Right knowledge begins with a flash of perception that makes us realize that no detail of our personal experience can be separated from the total expression of the One Life's activity.

This flash of realization, however brief, overthrows the idea of a separate personal will and disrupts the mental structures based on the error that we are living our lives in perpetual antagonism to the universe and to the lives of our neighbors. This lie is the basis for all the murders committed. This idea is eradicated by even the briefest perception of the fundamental unity of all that exists.

The falling figures represent the two modes of personal consciousness. The man is self-consciousness and the woman subconsciousness. This flash of inspiration upsets all our previous concepts of the nature of personal consciousness and reverses our former ways of thinking. Furthermore, they are wearing clothes, symbols of shame and sin. They hide both the aspects of consciousness, male and female, and their true natures from each other. By so doing, they remain in a state of ignorant separateness.

There are twenty-two Yods, tongues or flames of fire, which display the ten emanations on the Tree of Life and the twelve signs of the zodiac. They demonstrate that the sum total of cosmic forces do not have a physical foundation. The average individual believes that life has a physical basis. He also supposes that food, air, water and the forces of the environment sustain him. Ageless Wisdom declares, however, that the One Life is the basis of all manifestations and that the physical plane is the expression of the powers of spiritual life.

During this stage of unfoldment, the light is not continuous yet can never be forgotten. This recollection causes a fundamental concept to be formed as the basis for conducting life. It is the destiny of every soul to pass through such an experience for this terrible, sudden and wonderful awakening ends, definitively, the dream of separation. The aspirant is now ready to embark along the Path of Return.

The directional attribution of the Tower is North. It is the place in the Masonic Lodge where there are no stations. It is said that the sun never shines on the north side of Solomon's Temple. This is a reference to the black pillar between which the High Priestess sits. The idea behind this association between darkness and North is that those powers that are veiled in darkness are the powers, which bring release and enlightenment. Ageless Wisdom describes darkness as light too bright for the uninitiated to behold, which is therefore interpreted as darkness. The candidate, like all mankind, enters the Lodge or Planet Earth from the East, the direction of Light, and journeys to the West, the place of material experiences. In his journey back to the East he must return by way of North, the direction of the unknown, of the mysteries of life, and also of man's greatest fears. It is said that, "he who conquers his fear of darkness is able to discover the secrets it hides in order to bring them and himself to light."[12]

Key 3: The Empress　　　　*Key 10: Wheel of Fortune*　　　　*Key 17: The Star*

The third stage on the Path of Return is that of Multiplication and Creative Imagery. It represents the way multiplication manifests itself in our mental life. The symbol for multiplication and creative imagination is the Empress, Key 3. She represents the planet Venus, the direction East and she is pregnant. She is the result of the impregnation of subconscious by the impulses or seed ideas originating from self-consciousness. She is the Great Mother, pregnant with the world of form and thus represents the inner aspect of the process that establishes order. She is the woman spoken of in the Book of Revelation as having the twelve stars on her head and the Moon under her feet. The understanding of her symbolism and this principle in nature are essential to man's liberation. Ageless Wisdom teaches that it is the return of the feminine principle to an equal position of power that will accomplish the goal of victory toward which mankind journeys. The completion of the Great Work is the signal of that Victory. It is a victory that can only be accomplished by the

Sun and the Moon, with the aid of Mercury. The Moon is the basis of her power and it is the symbol for the rhythms and cycles, which influences the development of all kinds of growth, reproduction and imagination. The third stage emerges out of the bondage and imprisonment of ignorant separation and deluded thinking evidenced in Keys 15 and 16. Here, we see the woman in her rightful position of power wearing a crown of stars, symbolic of dominion, and holding her scepter of rulership. Only when the feminine occupies this position of power and equality in the life of the aspirant, and also in the life of humanity as a whole, can s/ he receive the Revelation of Isis-Urania.[13]

Acting through the agency of Key 10, the Wheel of Fortune or Rotation, the principle of multiplication leads to revelation. Key 10 is the symbol for the planet Jupiter, the planet of expansion on all levels of existence. Jupiter is said to be the god of clouds, rain and lightning. Under the law of Rotation, Jupiter, the planet of Great Fortune, accomplishes the work of wealth and achievement in the physical, emotional and mental planes, through the work of multiplication and growth, which are symbolized by the Empress.

The Empress brings all things into manifestation by the circulation of the root matter, water, represented by the Moon. A physical form can be thought of as the condensation of the electromagnetic "rain." It is this root matter, which pervades all space and veils the fiery energy of the One Force. This root matter with its interior fire is the alchemical water of which occultists speak. Through the process of spiral rotation, not circular, the activities of the One Force, makes all growth and evolution possible. This spiral motion appears to return to its starting point after each revolution, however, after each revolution, it actually begins at a higher level of rotation. It is the law of spiral rotation that is concerned with growth, involution, evolution, action and reaction, as well as the reciprocal relation that exists between the members of every pair of opposites throughout the universe. This law of rotation is at work in all cosmic manifestations and the Wheel of Fortune symbolizes it. The Jupiter center in the body is the epigastric plexus called the solar plexus. Its most important ganglia, is the semi-lunar ganglion, sometimes called the abdominal brain. It controls all of the abdominal viscera and has command over assimilation. There is a hint here to the combined work of the digestive process in illumination. The stomach is associated with the sign of Cancer, which is ruled by the Moon, and is also the sign in which Jupiter is exalted. Through the alchemical work in this Moon center, man is able to control the Law of Karma that is the consequence of the spiral rotation of cosmic cycles. Thereby, he can change the direction of his own fate and also the destiny of humanity.[14]

The Star, Key 17, also represents the third stage of unfoldment and is the symbol for the air sign of Aquarius. The nude Water-Bearer in the Key is Isis-Urania. The Hebrew name is Tzaddi and means fishhook; it alludes to the fishing or probing for solutions in the universal mind-stuff, or in the root matter, water. This is accomplished through meditation. This Yellow Star is the same Blazing Star found in the Masonic tradition. It is the Quintessence, or fifth essence of the alchemist, that is Spirit. There is a reference to the Star being that of Sirius in esoteric numerology. When the number seventeen is reduced, it yields the number eight, which is the number of the sign Leo and is associated with Sirius, which is a water planet. It is the guiding influence of this Star that will lead all mankind to find the solutions for all the problems of the world. The universal solvent is the human consciousness, concentrated and directed in meditation. The two vases she uses represent the two modes of consciousness, self-conscious and subconscious. Another name for this stage of enlightenment is Revelation. It is one of discovery, disclosure and unveiling. The seeker does not make the discovery of truth but rather it is made to him. He receives the revelation. He does not lift the veil of Isis; instead, she unveils herself to him. What the seeker seeks is Divine Order or that which is the true "kingdom of heaven within." When that order is found within the seeker, he can then find expression of that order in all things. Revelation comes when the mind has been made still, and the process of the principles and work of the previous stages, seals the senses. Disclosures made at this stage are not perceived by the physical senses, for the aspirant is on a quest for something that he cannot define. He is groping, feeling and fishing for something he feels he does not yet know. It is a means of trying to discover a secret and he is looking for a method whereby one can follow a clue leading to the understanding of a mystery. Because the WORD is seated in man's heart, he is able to receive its disclosure of truth within him. The method for this discovery is called Meditation, another name for Key 17.

A great sage defines meditation as "an unbroken flow of knowledge on a particular subject." It is the fishing and divining down into the depths of the stilled mind for the various associations connected with the main thought with which the seeker is concerned. Through the application of attention, association and mental imagery, revelation comes. When the thoughts are purified and concentrated, the whirling forces are synchronized and a rhythm is established which attunes the seeker to the greater rhythm of the Cosmic Order. Consequently, poise and balance are established because the personality vehicle is now attuned and in perfect alignment with the rhythms of Mother Nature, who Isis symbolizes in this Key. She demonstrates that meditation has a physical basis and she does so by resting one leg on land while balancing herself with the other foot that rests on the surface of the water. When we achieve stillness, we participate in the eternal cosmic meditation, which lifts the veil that hides the beautiful perfection of the Divine Mother.

The work of meditation is achieved in the body by the movement of the serpent force in the Scorpio region of the body. When this force is raised it becomes active in the Taurus regions, which are the hearing centers of the brain. The resulting stimulation of these centers enables the aspirant to become aware of the Inner Voice represented by the Hierophant. The true Revealer is the Inner Teacher or Hierophant and Key 17 is the symbol of that revelation.

The Fool and the World represent Uranus and Saturn, the first and the last of the twenty-two Keys, respectively, and collectively they rule Aquarius. These two symbols of the Fool and Saturn intimate that through meditation, man can find the solution to all his problems, from the most abstract, symbolized by the Fool, to the most concrete symbolized by Saturn, The World.[15]

Key 4: The Emperor   *Key 11: Justice*   *Key 18: The Moon*

The fourth stage of enlightenment is Organization. It is the principle of the fourth stage of unfoldment and is symbolized by the consort of the Empress, the Emperor. She establishes inner order while he establishes order in the outer world. Inner order must first be established before one can hope to achieve outer order. The fourth principle establishes the "squaring of the circle" by *earthing* Spirit in matter. The Emperor, the pictorial representation of Key 4, is the numeric symbol for the plane of matter. He represents the sign of Aries, which rules the head, face and perceptory function of sight, one of the attributes assigned to the Emperor. The Sun is exalted in this sign. The Emperor is an executive - one who sets things in order. He is the Magician and also an extension of the High Priestess by the fact that when the two are added or multiplied it gives us his number, four. Reason is an expression of memory. He also embodies the principles of the Magician and the Empress, numerically: one plus three. His sovereignty and rulership is dependent upon the motherhood of his consort, the Empress, just as her motherhood depends on him. Unless the universal subconscious brings forth a universe, the cosmic self-consciousness has nothing to govern. In this fourth stage of enlightenment, the order and administration of divine consciousness is and must be established in the body of the aspirant for the anchoring of God in form.

The exaltation of the Sun in Aries indicates that in this sign the highest expression of the solar energy is manifested. Under the rulership of Mars, the primal force is established in the body and gives tone to the muscular system through its action on the brain. All of the functions and powers in the body are the result of transforming solar energy in the cells of the human brain. This is accomplished by the transformation of this energy into rates of vibration which enable the personal consciousness to receive ideas, present in Universal Mind, which are being broadcast continuously throughout space. Just as the radio is not the originator of the thoughts it is able to pick up, neither is the brain the source of the information it receives. The brain, however, provides the necessary conditions for the expression of the thought.

The Emperor in man represents sovereign reason. He is the Founder of all things, and the framer of the universal constitution. Through human personality, the universal constituting power is made manifest by man's ability to see through outer appearances into the real nature of his environment. It is this vision in man that allows the Spirit in man to become aware of the universe. Reason, logic, correct vision, as well as the ability to measure and set boundaries are all essential to harmonious living. They put the individual in alignment with the One Mind for the remembrance, unfoldment and establishment of the god he is in form.[16]

Through the agency of Divine Justice symbolized by the lady Libra who carries the scales and the sword, the fourth stage of growth becomes a reality while still in the human form. The number representing the sign Libra is "11" (eleven) and means, esoterically, equilibrium or balance, the basis of the Great Work. The planet Venus is its natural ruler and Saturn is exalted in Libra or the sign of balance. Libra, the seventh sign of the zodiac, governs the kidneys, which is the organ that maintains the chemical equilibrium in the blood by eliminating waste. Proper functioning of the kidneys contributes to establishing proper emotional balance. The sword, one of the symbols of Libra, is used in the act of "cutting off" something; it, therefore, symbolizes the physical and mental eliminative process. The sword is also a symbol for the mind and so it represents the correct use of the mind in proper discrimination to rid oneself of everything that is useless, thereby, freeing the self from attachment, prejudice, resentment and regret.

The scale she holds gives us a clue to the achievement of balance in the human form. It represents the act of weighing and measuring through the exercise of mental powers and is related to mathematics. The two pans represent the equilibration of the 11 pairs of complementary activities. They correspond to the twenty-two Tarot Keys and the twenty-two letters of the Hebrew alphabet. Additionally, the length of the crossbar of the scales is the same as the lines supporting the pans showing seven equal lines. They represent the seven aspects of the Life Power represented by Keys 1, 2, 3, 10, 16, 19 and 21. These keys represent the seven chakras or wheels of force in the body, as well as the seven planets: Mercury, the Moon, Venus, Jupiter, Mars, the Sun and Saturn that are related to them. These seven bodies also correspond to the seven alchemical metals: Mercury or Quicksilver, Silver, Copper, Tin, Steel, Gold and Lead, respectively. It is through the balancing and alignment of these seven centers that the expression of the One Life Force is expressed in the body.[17]

Again, Organization, the sign of Pisces, Key 18, and the Moon symbolize the fourth stage of unfoldment. Jupiter and Neptune rule this sign with the planet Venus in exaltation. The Hebrew name is Qoph and Qabalah assigns it to "Sleep" and the back of the head or sleep center. The aspirant has now experienced the turbulence of Keys 15 and 16, which shattered his world of illusion, which was based on his bondage to separateness and the confusion and isolation of wrong thought and action. In the quietness and rest of Key 17, through meditation, new relationships are revealed to him, the traveler, in search of truth. He is now ready for the process of Organization. Beware, this does not mean group formation.

The structures in the human body are being re-organized into a higher type of human organism. This spontaneous evolutionary process brings man to the point of being human and, along with the development of the brain structures he accommodates the use of the divine principles, for his further development toward self-realization. Returning to Key 18, out of the pool, the symbol of the great deep, cosmic mind-stuff emerges in the shape of a scorpion onto the dry land of physical manifestation. The scorpion is a reference to the Scorpio energy that rises and activates the journey of the Path of Return.

The Path out of the pool traverses over rolling terrain and between two towers before they reach to the mountaintop of spiritual attainment. This is a reference to the waxing and waning cycles of the Moon and also the need in human activities for periods of assimilation and elimination, for periods of intense effort alternated by periods of rest and relaxation. The "place" of the towers represents the ordinary limits of human perception and attainment, but the distance between the towers and the mountaintop symbolizes the vast region to be explored and conquered by the aspirant within himself and nature. The Towers represent a doorway or an opening and is a reference to Daleth "the door or opening." Creative Imagination provides a portal to what lies beyond his ordinary senses. Man alone is capable of self-modification. This is not accomplished by selection and breeding. It is by the direct action of man's will and imagination upon his own vehicle of flesh and blood that the transformation is effected. Man is not only the operator but also the subject in the Great Work. Transformation is the outcome of the working together of universal forces because the human factor is an essential component of it. No man can accomplish this work, however, until he himself sees, understands and applies the principles, laws and forces, which are involved in the transformation of his own substance. This process is alchemically called "the Operation of the Sun."

The production of new organs in the body is a result of the supervening of a new "want" continuing to make itself felt, as well as a new movement which this "want" gives birth to, and encourages. This effort must, for the most part, be conscious. It must be made with the mental intent of producing some desirable result. This is how mankind gives birth to a new self and a new species of himself.

The exaltation of Venus the Great Mother, symbolic of the deep ocean and the root matter, gives us a hint to what Qabalists say concerning the Sun and its thirty-two rays, sixteen principal and sixteen secondary. First, in the heart of the Son-Sun (Man) are to be found the sources of beauty. Second, it is in the aspect of the Life Power identified in alchemy as the "white work" of the Moon, that is concealed the real secret of building the mystical temple of regenerated humanity. A hint is given here to the Moon centers in the body! The thirty-two paths of wisdom, alluded to in the thirty-second degree of the Masonic tradition, is a concrete achievement at the cellular level of the body and not gained through social and monetary contributions or long-standing memberships.

If our patterns are clear and definite, they are passed into the subconscious where they build a body corresponding to these patterns. Most of the important organs of the brain are located at the rear of the scull, where the posterior lobes of the cerebrum and cerebellum are situated. We, in fact, see with the back of the head via the cerebrum that houses the sight center. The medulla oblongata, a knot of nerve tissues at the back of the head, unites the brain to the spinal cord and its other nerve branches. It is the connecting link between the higher centers of sensation, thought and action, which are located in the head and the lower centers located in the lower part of the body. It is during sleep that aspirations and efforts are built into organic structures. This is so because our mental processes continue at the subconscious levels while the cells of the upper brain rest during sleep. The path of return is not one of acquiring power or becoming spiritual.

It is the way of conscious return to what we really are, for it progressively develops the skills necessary for the exercise of our powers. "Matter" is the way in which the One Spirit manifests itself within the range of our senses. Every cell is Pure Spirit and that is why our bodies are truly the temples of God.[18]

Key 5: The Hierophant   *Key 12: Hanged Man*   *Key 19: The Sun*

Intuition is the principle that marks the fifth stage of unfoldment called Regeneration. Intuition is symbolized by the Hierophant, Key 5, which represents the sign of Taurus under the planetary rulership of Venus, in which the Moon is exalted. The Hierophant and the Emperor are one and the same. The Emperor in us is a symbol of earthly rulership, while the Hierophant symbolizes spiritual dominion and thereby represents a human upon whom spiritual sovereignty has been bestowed. He is the Master Mason of Masonic tradition. The Hierophant is the symbol of the Inner Teacher or Inner Voice called intuition. Intuition is defined as interior teaching. It is the direct perception of eternal principles that may be applied to the solution of human problems and to the perfecting of human control over his environment. This direct perception is the result of the union of personal consciousness with the Central Self. The Hierophant is the revealer of mysteries and the teacher of the sacred symbols. Intuition is the extension and natural progression from reason, but it is NOT a substitute for reason. No one can "hear" his inner teacher until he has developed the ability to think logically, rationally and objectively, or rather, not until the principles of reasoning are established in him. He must have first trained his mental vision in order to be able to see his situation clearly. Intuition is also not to be confused with hunches and psychic impressions. True intuition always unfolds principles. Some ways of distinguishing the inner "VOICE" is that it never flatters, nor does it ever make promises of wealth, power, knowledge or prominence. In fact, it never speaks to the individual until he has achieved mental quietness in his life. The two acolytes kneeling in humility at the feet of the inner teacher are surrendering the intellectual and emotional knowledge of what they think they know, so that they can be taught the divine principles. When the principle of the inner teacher is applied, a reversal of consciousness in the individual is brought about.[19]

The agent through which the Inner Teacher achieves regeneration in man is called "the Hanged Man", Key 12, which is symbolized by the planet Neptune, representative of water and also the Law of Reversal. This law finds expression in the mental attitudes of the very wise, the very opposite of popular opinion. Water symbolizes reversal because it reflects everything upside down. Water is the symbol for subconscious, both personal and universal. It is the substance of every form in the Universe. It is the One Thing from which all things are made. This "matter" of subconsciousness which seems to be so dense, hard and mentally impenetrable by the average individual, is known by practical occultists to be made up of "drops" of alchemical "water". The occultist knows that there is no difference between the energy, which takes form as thought, and the thought, which takes form as a solid object. In their view, thought-forms are more intense and have longer lasting activity than physical things.

The scientific conception of the electrical constitution of matter is the same as the occult teaching regarding water as substance. This understanding enables the aspirant to effect a total reversal in his interpretation of his environment, and through this reversal he is able to free his mind from the subjection to appearances, which prevents him from using mental imagery to change his conditions for the better. The Hanged Man symbolizes the suspension of personal mental activity, achieved through concentration. The personality vehicle then becomes the indispensable agent whereby the powers of the One Life are expressed in the conditions of relative existence. This state of being or Divine Consciousness is reached due to the chemical changes in the composition of the blood. These changes can only be effected from within the body organism and not by outside agencies or the use of drugs.

During a state of mental reversal, personal particulars are reduced to a minimum and emphasis falls on the Inner Self or the true Spiritual Identity. To reverse one's mental attitude is to have a new world-view that sees the universe as a dance of life: full of joy and freedom. One also realizes that the Life-Power is the basis of all forms. At the center of every human personality is this pure divine essence, which is known as the God spark in man. Practice with this knowledge will bring about a reversal in common interpretations.

The fifth stage of unfoldment is a result of the progressive work of the principles in the human organism. In this stage, symbolized by the Sun, Key 19, the new birth from natural humanity to spiritual humanity takes place. The powers of subconsciousness in the natural man have been stifled and perverted due to his implantation of erroneous conscious thinking. By applying the divine principles to his conscious thinking, he becomes a new man and so "twice born". In this process of transformation, he has carried out the injunction of the scriptures, which commands, "be ye transformed by the renewing of your minds".

This new birth includes alterations in the physical and emotional bodies of the aspirant. In this is a deep inner realization of man's place in the cosmic order. The fifth stage of unfoldment is a grade of adeptship and a stage of conscious identification with the One Identity. The point of entrance for the radiant energy of the Sun, into the human body and also into the field of personality, is through a group of nerve cells called the cardiac ganglion located in the sympathetic nervous system above and behind the heart. The Life-Power enters the body here just as an electrical current enters a building at the main switch. The nerve cells of this sun center charge the blood stream with this radiant energy as it passes through the heart. One of the consequences of occult training is the development of finer vision along with the ability to see these fine vibrations or this force as it enters the body through this "main switch." The Sun is the ruler of the sign of Leo, which governs the heart. This confirms Ageless Wisdom's attribution of the sun to the cardiac ganglion.[20]

The picture in Key 19 with the human features on the solar disk are intended to show that this is a living conscious intelligence as well as a synthesis of all the active forces entering into the composition of human personality. Of the five sunflowers shown, four are open, showing the full development of the four kingdoms of nature: mineral, vegetable, animal and human. The fifth sunflower is partially opened because it represents a stage of development not yet experienced by most of humanity. This is the symbol of the kingdom of spiritual humanity, which is composed of regenerated men and women. The anatomical structures of these beings are the same as humans however only when the spiritual eyes are opened can men recognize them even though they live among men.

The two children in the fairy ring are of the same height and the same size because they allude to the childlike and transparent nature of the "twice born". They are nude because self-consciousness and subconsciousness have nothing to conceal from each other. Here, nature is unveiling itself as truth. Their words and their lives are simple and yet, because they are so plain and direct, what they say is seldom understood.

The establishment of consciousness in the organism for communication with the Higher Self takes place through the influx of the All, Key 0, into the field of self-consciousness symbolized by Key 1. It is directed to subconscious levels in order to modify the operations of the serpent or Scorpio force. In so doing, the Magician cultivates flowers in his garden. Again, flowers are the reproductive organs of the vegetable kingdom. This Scorpio force, raised for the purpose of awakening the brain centers, brings the aspirant into a higher order of knowing, but under correct guidance. What results is a physiological and psychological transformation. The adept's body is bio-chemically changed, as are the subtle structures of his cells, thus making him a newly born or regenerated being.[21]

Key 6: The Lovers   Key 13: Death   Key 20: Judgment

The sixth stage of unfoldment is symbolized by Key 20 and is the pen-ultimate stage of enlightenment represented by the planet Pluto, Divine Fire. The principle active at this stage is that of Discrimination, symbolized by the Lovers, Key 6 and ruled by the planet Mercury. It is also representative of the zodiacal sign of Gemini, the Twins. The Hebrew name for this Key is Zain which means sword, an instrument of cleavage which is able to make clear, sharp divisions. The power of discrimination is the ability to perceive differences. Additionally, it is the basis for self-consciousness since it is only through the self-conscious mind that things are perceived as many seemingly unrelated parts, instead of as a single unity. These apparently unrelated realities are all reflections of the One Reality. This ability to discern and to make clear distinctions makes the sense of smell an appropriate attribution for Key 6. The angel pictured here is Archangel Raphael, which is super-consciousness and the ruler of the element of air. He is called "God the Healer of Mind". He represents the idea that, right discrimination leads to the recognition of the Unity of the One, and that true healing is the attainment of wholeness of both the inner and outer through the union with the One Self.

The woman in the Key is Eve, spoken of in the Bible, and corresponds to the Empress and the High Priestess. Behind her is the tree of the Knowledge of Good and Evil around which is wrapped the Serpent or Scorpio force. This force or vibration is what at first leads us into temptation through delusion. It is the same force, which delivers us from evil when through right discrimination we learn how to apply it in order to overcome our errors in thinking. The tree bears five fruits. They are our five senses through which we experience the physical plane and they also represent the five elements: ether, fire, water, air and earth. Eve is the mother of all creation and the symbol of subconsciousness and all its activities.

Behind the man is a tree whose twelve leaves are flames; each of them has three parts. They represent the twelve signs of the zodiac with their three decanate or sub-divisions, thereby, symbolizing the thirty-six sub-types of human personality. The journey of enlightenment is consciousness journeying through the twelve signs and thirty-six sub-types of the zodiac.

The man and the woman are nude and are not ashamed of it because in right discrimination, self- consciousness conceals nothing of its own nature from itself. Henceforth, they have nothing to hide. They are the same height and the same size because self-consciousness has created the correct premises that will allow sub-consciousness to accurately reflect and carry out the will of super-consciousness. Subconsciousness is the body-builder and the ruler of the complex chemical and electrical functions of the organism. An inevitable consequence of this is that through the work of subconsciousness, the whole organism will be so adjusted that the healing work of Archangel Raphael can be realized for all life.

Realization, the sixth stage of unfoldment, is based on the principle of discrimination and works through the agency of Death or Transformation symbolized by Key 13, the sign of Scorpio. Scorpio is ruled by Mars, Pluto and Uranus, is exalted. The very name of this Key suggests dissolution and change. Death, however, is the basis for evolution and without death, change and re-birth could not occur. Scorpio is the sign that governs the reproductive organs, indicating that the force used in reproduction has to do with the liberating transformation of dissolution. Mars is said to be the ruler of both Aries and Scorpio. Aries rules the head and the brain. Aries is known as the day throne of Mars and Scorpio, the night throne. When the Mars force, working under darkness and concealment of Scorpio, is used by occult practice under right supervision, the brain centers ruled by Aries are energized. The aspirant is brought into the daylight of the clear vision of reality, represented by the Emperor.

Additionally, Uranus, the planet representing super-consciousness is shown symbolically as the white rose, meaning purified desire, the Fool, Key 0. The influence of Uranus allows mankind to experience first-hand the knowledge of immortality. The rising sun coming up over the eastern horizon makes reference to the

Empress as well as the dawn or birth of a new consciousness as a result of the understanding and application of the principle and agency of water. Through the correct action of Key 13 in the body, mankind has the opportunity to learn the deep secrets of life in order to gain the inheritance from his great wise brothers who walked this very road. Hint: Scorpio rules the eighth house of death and inheritance. Life and death are truly two aspects of the same force applied under the agency of Love and Power for the continuation of more and exalted living.[22]

Realization during the sixth stage of unfoldment brings the adept to the verge of merging with universal consciousness where he knows that in reality the personality has no separate existence. His intellectual conviction is confirmed by his fourth dimensional experience, the phenomenon, which will forever end the delusion of separateness. He has now come to know factually that: "I have no will, but to do the will of Him that sent me". Key 20 is the symbol for this stage of realization and is represented by the Archangel of the Moon, Gabriel. He sounds a trumpet, which causes the dead to rise from their coffins floating on a sea. It is the human personality, which is being thus raised from the death of the three-dimensional consciousness by the power descending from above rather than the efforts of the personality from below. The seven rays coming from the trumpet make reference to the seven chakras of Key 17 and also to the fact that awakening to higher consciousness is accompanied by sound.

The three figures are that of self-consciousness, subconsciousness and the regenerated man, represented by the "Christ child". It is the same reference to Osiris, Isis and Horus, the Egyptian triad. Their nudity suggests intimacy, innocence and a freedom from shame and the false notions of incorrect thinking. Their skin is gray to suggest that they have achieved the required balance over all the pairs of opposites and they, therefore, rise out of the coffins. They are on the sea, which is the symbol of subconsciousness and the Great Mother. The sea is the end of flowing water and this symbolism is suggesting an end or termination, called Judgment, or a reasoned and comprehensive conclusion. Judgment is also the end of reasoning and, at this point, a new order of knowing is manifested. There is no more weighing of evidence, no more discussion of pros and cons, no more arguments for, and against.

Old things are passed away and all things have become as new. This judgment is a decision that terminates forever the connection with the false knowledge of this world. It also terminates our sense of mortality.

Unlike the lightning flash of Key 16, the adept never again returns to ignorance. The adept is free from the lapses of memory he experienced earlier on his journey. With this new consciousness, he sleeps no more though his body may rest. He is able to function consciously in the fourth dimension so that he may "serve God day and night" in the ranks of his Great Companions. The great secret of those who have attained this level of unfoldment cannot be told. To tell it would be pointless because it would not be believed. So, when they speak, it is not for imparting the secret, but to point out the way.

Key 20 suggests the union of the divine spark in man with the totality of the Divine Being. This is a direct consequence of conscious attunement of the personal will to the intellectually recognized Divine Will. The only constant unchanging reality is Pure Spirit. When mankind rids himself of his reliance on things and circumstances and rests himself on the only sure foundation of eternal being, he will begin to live. Things always fail when one makes them the foundation of ones life because things are ephemeral and will always pass away. However, the largest number of humanity, since the history of our planet, has done the work necessary to prepare themselves. They are now responding to the sound of Archangel Gabriel's trumpet to be "awake" forever and never fall asleep again, thereby conquering the last enemy called Death.[23]

Key 7: The Chariot   *Key 14: Temperance*   *Key 21: The World*

Key 21 symbolizes the seventh and, final stage of enlightenment known as Cosmic Consciousness. This principle is that of Receptivity symbolized by Key 7, which works through the agency of Temperance, Key 14, to complete the journey of the soul in form.

One of the attributions assigned to the Chariot, also referred to as Fence, Key 7, by the Qabalah, is Intelligence of the House of Secret Influences. The Moon rules this Key and it represents the sign of Cancer in which Jupiter is exalted. As the Crab, the symbol for Cancer, carries its house on its back, the personality vehicle is the house in which the SELF lives. The Rider is the True Self who rides in the Chariot we call our personality vehicle that is built by the subconscious aspect of Being. Personality is a "Chariot" projected into form by the One Self in order to be a vehicle with which the One Self may experience this physical dimension.

What is important to grasp, therefore, is that the personality has no will of its own. The occultist knows that "Will" is not something that strong-minded people possess and the timid are devoid of. Will is the motivating power behind the entire universe. It is that quality which every person and thing in creation has an equal share of. The difference lies in the degree of each individual's ability to express that Will through his personality.

As shown in Key 6 on discrimination, the Source of Will Power is behind and above the two modes of human consciousness. Human personality is the dwelling place of the power that flows into the conscious and subconscious levels of personality from the plane above those levels. Individuals who possess that master-consciousness, as well as, the mental state, which permit the greatest possible expression of Will- Power and the highest degree of control over circumstances, are also those who grasp a great truth. The field of personality, suggested by the Key, must be cultivated and the master cultivator is the Inner Self. The potencies of Will Power can then be brought into active manifestation through the functions of the personal vehicle that has been prepared.

The Hebrew word for Key 7 is Cheth and in Qabalah is related to the function of speech, whether audible or silent thoughts. Through our speech, we give clues to the patterns of our life-expressions and to our physical, emotional and mental states. Words have specific vibratory powers and are in themselves words of power related to sound. Key 7, the Chariot, answers the fundamental questions of whom and what we are. We now know that the true personality is cultivated and is a moving Intelligent House of Influence in the physical universe. Thus, the meanings of victory, wealth and abundance express adequately the state of consciousness achieved by the Rider, the Reconciler of the two contending forces pictured by the two sphinxes.[24]

Through the agency of Archangel Michael symbolized by Temperance, Key 14, the work achieved so far is verified. This Key is ruled by Jupiter and represents the fiery sign of Sagittarius, which has to do with "travel into strange and distant countries." The longing in the human heart is that which leads man away from the world of false appearances into the country which, although to many might seem strange, is his true home. The symbols of the Eagle and the Lion refer to the Scorpio and Leo regions of the body, which are the reproductive and heart centers, respectively. Their combined function in the body, under the initiating function of Archangel Michael, ignites the light in the head, symbolized by the Crown at the end of the Path. This path leads the aspirant out of the pool of unconsciousness back into conscious union with the Self, thus completing the Great Work.

The seven-pointed star on the angel's breast is a symbol of mastery. It is a figure that must be drawn by experimenting with a pair of compass and requires skill, indicating that the aspirant must participate fully and consciously in the process of his own unfoldment. A compass, according to freemasonry, means to "circumscribe our desires and keep our passions in due bounds." It is, therefore, a symbol for the control of the fiery forces of desire. The Great Work is the adaptation of the skills of the magical art to the transformation of the personality and to the raising or expansion of consciousness until the individual is able to perceive clearly the laws and principles by which they operate. Through the influence of the principle of verification, the aspirant for initiation puts himself through tests and trials in the refining fire of life's circumstances. No one ever attains mastery without sacrifice. Those who know the value of his objective, feels no sense of loss when he rids himself of every encumbrance that interferes with his progress.

The Hebrew word for Key 14 is Samekh, which represents trial, probation, purgation and purification of the personality for the sole objective of making him a fit channel for the expression of the One

Force. He becomes a fit Temple of the Most High, a pure and holy habitation for the One Spirit. By so doing, the Law of Verification brings about the establishment of the House of God. It is important here to realize that Archangel Michael is the Devil of Key 15, but without the mask. He is also the Hierophant of Key 5. It is he who is spoken of in the Scriptures to whom the keys of heaven and hell are given. He is MAN, the Great Mystery, who is also his own Redeemer![25]

Cosmic Consciousness is the final stage of enlightenment and is symbolized by Key 21 and ruled by the planet Saturn. It is indeed world consciousness, the attainment of the consciousness of the whole world. This is the state of Nirvana that gives the attained firsthand knowledge of his identity with the One Power, which is the source of all that governs and directs the entire manifested universe. Words are inadequate to describe the idea of what the pictorial tries to convey as the Eternal Dancer, the Adept and universal Dance of Life.

The wreath, which is the work of man, is composed of a twenty-two triad of leaves where each triad corresponds to one of the Hebrew letters and to the twenty-two aspects of consciousness and modes of the Life Force. Each mode of consciousness has three expressions: integrative, disintegrative and equilibrating. The latter balances the former two, a fact demonstrated by the spirals in her hands. Nature provides the leaves, but it is man who weaves them into a chaplet for the Victor. It is, therefore, a symbol of man's capacity to adapt the forces of nature. It also suggests that cosmic consciousness is not spontaneously provided for by natural evolution, but that the completion of the Great Work is a result of the great artistry of man. The two "figure eights" at the top and bottom of the wreath indicate that the forces of Tau, the Hebrew letter name for Key 21 are those used by man to bind together the forces of nature, which form the wreath.

The number twenty-one is the sum of the numbers from zero to six and, therefore, shows the completion or the extension of the powers of the principles represented by these numbers. Saturn, or the Hebrew name Shabbathai, means Sabbath. It is the seventh planet and is the day of rest known by Ageless Wisdom as Sabbath, a time when the aspirant rests from his labors.

Tau means mark, signature or seal in the form of an equal armed cross where the point at the center is the dwelling place of the One Identity. This mark is a symbol of validity, completion of the Great Work and salvation from death. It is also the signature of eternal life. It is this Center in the Heart, the Palace of the King, where the One Self is enthroned. It is a central point of authority and rulership that gives this mode of consciousness the attribution of Administrative Intelligence. It is this intelligence, which directs the operation of the seven interior planets and their activities and guides them all in their proper course.[26] These seven planets are the seven double letters used by freemasonry to define God as: height, Mercury (Key 1); depth, the Moon (Key 2); east, Venus, the Empress (Key 3); west, Jupiter (Key 10); north, Mars (Key 16); south, the Sun (Key 19); and CENTER, the Holy Temple, Saturn (Key 21).[27]

The four animals in the four corners of the Key are those of the four fixed signs of Leo, Scorpio, Aquarius and Taurus representing the four elements of fire, water, air and earth. These are the four fixed signs which make up the fixed cross on which the error of personality domination is forever crucified.

The Dancer is perfectly free and has always been, and is a Celestial Androgyne. The Dancer stands on nothing, is self-supported, is in perfect equilibrium, and now has dominion over the laws, which in the past had served to bind. This is no longer so, for no law binds the SELF!

It is my hope that you too consciously unfold the Dancer you already are.

Afterword

We are now at the dawn of a glorious future. One in which we will know, firsthand, from the depth of our beings, the glory of the decision and choice we made in that now dim and distant past. That decision was to go on a new adventure into form. It was the promise of this New Age wherein we will remember who and what we are, as well as, what is our place of origin. We are at the end of the Piscean experience, which was marked by division, separateness and war. On the other hand, however, we saw great accomplishments in education, the development of the mind and a deep desire for peace made poignant by the World Wars and the many cultural, religious and racial conflicts.

We are embarking on a new adventure in which science will penetrate the depth of matter to reveal to humanity the presence of Spirit that it holds. Likewise, the spiritual world will unveil its secret mysteries, which, in turn, will help mankind remember his origin and purpose here. All this will be facilitated by the power and rulership of Uranus; the planet of occultism and absolute unity. The scientific community will uncover and reveal the evidence of the absolute unity of all humanity and, all life. The mystery of fire, air, water, sound, color and light will be uncovered and this knowledge will help humanity to understand his true nature and his divine essence. The true relationship between the physical and the spiritual will be better understood.

The Masonic concept will become the foundation for understanding force and form and help concretize spirit in matter. Mankind will be powerfully moved along the evolutionary path toward the spiritual understanding of occultism as it builds on the beautiful mystical experience of the last 2,100 years. Mankind will construct a new structure based on the knowledge of ceremonial order and alchemy. The concrete knowledge of Man, which occultism provides, will add to his knowledge of the emotional and feeling nature of the mystical path he has traveled in the Age just ended. For a synthesis of this understanding, Masonry was given to us. The western mysteries will unveil the process of achieving full consciousness while living and working in the marketplace. Only then will we truly understand the relationship between matter and spirit.

The externalization of the Hierarchy in all of our systems of government will position these masters of wisdom to carry out the fulfillment of the divine Will to man. These Initiates are the connecting link between the kingdom of Spirit and the kingdom of Humanity. And, in their positions of power, they will ensure that the kingdoms of spirit and humanity become united and that this reality does not continue to be one of only hopes and dreams. I hold the vision with an awakening humanity for a New World in which there will not just be tolerance for each other's differences but a love and celebration based on the knowledge of our brotherhood and common ancestry.

Scientific and spiritual research will reveal the knowledge of the deep, cellular inter-connectedness and dependence on each other for our eventual individual and collective liberation from the grip of ignorance. Mankind will emerge out of the Aquarian experience with the knowledge of his greatness, that he is divine, sovereign and glorious. He will know without a doubt that he is both God and man and that each person's eyes he looks into, reflect the same glory he is, regardless of gender, color and culture.

Man will then know the reason for which he started this long journey, eons ago, to experience the grandeur of who he is while clothed in matter. He will become the ruler of air, water, fire and earth and in turn, become the reflected glory to all life on earth and to all the multi-universes everywhere. Let the Dance begin in earnest.

References

Chapter Zero: Introduction

[1]Bailey, Alice A., *Esoteric Astrology*, London: Lucis Press Ltd., 1951, p.349

[2]Ibid, p.350

[3]Wilmshurst, W.L., *The Meaning of Masonry*, London: Watkins Publishing Company, 1959, p. 43

[4]Bailey, Alice A., *Esoteric Astrology*, London: Lucis Press Ltd., 1951, p. 422

[5]Ibid, p.349

[6]Ibid, p.416

[7]Ibid, p.426

[8]Ibid, p.560

[9]Ibid, p.560

[10]Ibid, p.561

Chapter One

[1]Bailey, Alice A., *Esoteric Astrology*, London: Lucis Press Ltd., 1951, pp. 465-467

[2]Bailey, Alice A., *The Labours of Hercules: An Astrological Interpretation*, New York: Lucis Publishing Company, 1974, p.32

[3]Ibid, pp. 45-46

[4]Ibid, p.66

[5]Bailey, Alice A., *Esoteric Astrology*, London: Lucis Press Ltd., 1951, p.313

[6]Ibid, p.302

[7]Ibid, pp. 251-252

[8]Bailey, Alice A., *The Labours of Hercules: An Astrological Interpretation*, New York: Lucis Publishing Company, 1974, p.131

[9]Three Initiates, *The Kybalion*, Chicago: The Yogi Publication Society, Masonic Temple, 1940, p.179

[10]Bailey, Alice A., *Esoteric Astrology*, London: Lucis Publishing Company, 1951, p. 318-319

[11]Ibid, p.160

[12]Ibid, 172

[13]Bailey, Alice A., *The Labours of Hercules: An Astrological Interpretation*, New York: Lucis Publishing Company, 1974, p.185

[14]Bailey, Alice A., *Esoteric Astrology*, London: Lucis Publishing Company, 1951, p. 224

[15]Ibid, p. 168

[16]Bailey, Alice A., *The Labors of Hercules: An Astrological Interpretation*, New York: Lucis Publishing Company, 1974, p. 199

[17]Case, Paul Foster, *The Tarot: A Key to the Wisdom of the Ages*, Los Angeles: Builders of the Adytum, 1990, p.185

[18]Bailey, Alice A., *Esoteric Astrology*, London: Lucis Publishing Company, 1951, p. 413

[19]Ibid, p. 116

[20]Ibid, p. 214

Chapter Two

[1]Bailey, Alice A., *Esoteric Astrology*, London: Lucis Publishing Company, 1951, p. 352

[2]Ibid, p.208

[3]Bailey, Alice A., *The Labors of Hercules: An Astrological Interpretation*, New York: Lucis Publishing Company, 1974, p. 227

[4]Fortune, Dion, *The Mystical Kabalah*, Maine: Samuel Wiser Inc., 1984, pp. 32-33

[5]Ibid, p.110

[6]Ibid, 123

[7]Ibid, p.139

[8]Ibid, p.161

[9]Ibid, p.173

[10]Ibid, p.189

[11]Ibid, p.221

[12]Ibid, p.238

[13]Ibid, p.252

[14]Ibid, p.266

[15]Case, Paul Foster, *The Tarot: A Key to the Wisdom of the Ages*, Los Angeles: Builders of the Adytum, 1990, p.32

[16]Ibid, p.42

[17]Ibid, p.51

[18]Ibid, p.58

[19]Ibid, p.66

[20]Ibid, p.76

[21]Case, Paul Foster, *The Book of Tokens*, Los Angeles: Builders of the Adytum, 1989, p.75

[22]Case, Paul Foster, *The Tarot: A Key to the Wisdom of the Ages*, Los Angeles: Builders of the Adytum, 1990, p.99

[23]Ibid, p.104

[24]Ibid, p. 113

[25]Ibid, p. 121

[26]Ibid, p. 130

[27]Ibid, pp. 137-138

[28]Ibid, p. 146

[29]Ibid, pp. 157-158

[30]Case, Paul Foster, *The Book of Tokens,* Los Angeles: Builders of the Adytum, 1989, p.147

[31]Case, Paul Foster, *The Tarot: A Key to the Wisdom of the Ages*, Los Angeles: Builders of the Adytum, 1990, pp. 170-171

[32]Case, Paul Foster, *The Book of Tokens*, Los Angeles: Builders of the Adytum, 1989, p. 161

[33]Ibid, p. 169

[34]Case, Paul Foster, *The Tarot: A Key to the Wisdom of the Ages*, Los Angeles: Builders of the Adytum, 1990, p. 194

[35]Ibid, pp. 200-201

[36]Ibid, p. 206

[37]Fortune, Dion, *The Mystical Qabalah*, Maine: Samuel Wiser Inc., 1984, p. 298

Chapter Three

[1]Bailey, Alice A., *Esoteric Psychology*, vol.1, London: Lucis Publishing Company, 1951, p. 395

[2]Ibid, p. 397

[3]Ibid, p. 398

[4]Ibid, p. 399

[5]Ibid, p. 400

[6]Armstrong, Herbert W., *The United States and Britain in Prophecy*, Pasadena: Worldwide Church of God, 1980, pp. 28-29

[7]Ibid, p. 27

[8]Ibid, p. 36

[9]Bailey, Alice A., *Destiny of the Nations*, London: Lucis Press Ltd., 1952, p. 167

[10]Armstrong, Herbert W., *The United States and Britain in Prophecy*, Pasadena: Worldwide Church of God, 1980, p.58

[11]Ibid, pp. 33-34

[12]Hall, Manly P., *The Lost Keys of Freemasonry*, New York: Macoy Publishing and Masonic Supply Company, 1957, p. 35

[13]Wilmshurst, W. L., *The Meaning of Masonry*, London: Watkins Publishing Company, 1959, p. 29

[14]Ibid, p. 31

[15]Ibid, p. 32

[16] Hall, Manly P., *The Lost Keys of Freemasonry*, New York: Macoy Publishing and Masonic Supply Company, 1957, p. 35

[17]Wilmshurst, W. L., *The Meaning of Masonry*, London: Watkins Publishing Company, 1959, p. 107

References

[18]Ibid, p. 88

[19]Ibid, p. 135

[20]Ibid, p. 35

[21]Ibid, p. 39

[22]Ibid, p. 40

[23]Ibid, pp. 45-46

[24]Ibid, p. 47

[25]Bailey, Alice A., *Esoteric Astrology*, London: Lucis Publishing Company, 1951, p.394

[26]Ibid, pp. 169-170

[27]Ibid, p. 167

[28]Ibid, p. 396

[29]Ibid, p. 154

[30]Ibid, p. 530

[31]Bailey, Alice A., *The Externalization of the Hierarchy*, London: Lucis Publishing Company, 1951, pp. 126- 127

[32]Ibid, p. 132

Chapter Four

[1]Case, Paul Foster, *The Tarot: A Key to the Wisdom of the Ages*, Los Angeles: Builders of the Adytum, 1990, p.176

[2]Bailey, Alice A., *Esoteric Astrology*, London: Lucis Publishing Company, 1951, p. 296

[3]Blavatsky, H. P., *Secret Doctrine, vol.II*, Pasedena: Theosophical University Press, 1970, p.400

[4]Case, Paul Foster, *The Tarot: A Key to the Wisdom of the Ages*, Los Angeles: Builders of the Adytum, 1990, p.76

[5]Ibid, p. 44

[6]Ibid, p. 78

[7]Ibid, p. 31

[8] Ibid, p.42

[9]Ibid, p. 43

[10]Ibid, p. 45

[11]Ibid, p. 44

[12]Bailey, Alice A., *Esoteric Astrology*, London: Lucis Publishing Company, 1951, p. 386

[13]Case, Paul Foster, *The Tarot: A Key to the Wisdom of the Ages*, Los Angeles: Builders of the Adytum, 1990, p.51

[14]Bailey, Alice A., *Esoteric Astrology*, London: Lucis Publishing Company, 1951, p. 296

[15]Ibid, p. 297

[16]Ibid, p. 297

[17]Ibid, p. 385

[18]Ibid, p. 281

[19]Ibid, pp. 179-180

[20]Ibid, p. 446

[21]Bailey, Alice A., *Externalization of the Hierarchy*, London: Lucis Press Ltd., 1939, p. 37

[22]Ibid, p. 98

[23]Bailey, Alice A., *Esoteric Astrology*, London: Lucis Publishing Company, 1951, p. 444

[24]Ibid, p. 445

Chapter Five

[1]Blavatsky, H. P., *Secret Doctrine, vol.II*, Pasedena: Theosophical University Press, 1970, p. 232.

[2]Ibid, p. 272

[3]Ibid, p. 7

[4]Ibid, p. 273

[5]Ibid, p. 275

[6]Ibid, p. 272

[7]Bailey, Alice A., *Externalization of the Hierarchy*, London: Lucis Press Ltd., 1939, p.72

[8]Ibid, p. 273

[9]Ibid, p. 274

[10]Ibid, p. 120

[11]Bailey, Alice A., *Externalization of the Hierarchy*, London: Lucis Press Ltd., 1939, p.121

[12]Ibid, p. 123

[13]Ibid, p. 122

[14]Ibid, p. 519

[15]Ibid, p. 89

[16]Bailey, Alice A., *Esoteric Astrology*, London: Lucis Publishing Company, 1951, p. 207 [17]Bailey, Alice A., *Externalization of the Hierarchy*, London: Lucis Press Ltd., 1939, p. 89 [18]Ibid, p. 89

[19]Ibid, p. 669

[20]Ibid, p. 662

[21]Ibid, p. 657

[22]Ibid, p. 507

[23]Ibid, pp. 667-668

[24] Ibid, p.666

[25]Ibid, p. 87

[26]Ibid, p. 88

[27]Ibid, p. 100

[28]Ibid, pp. 77-78

[29]Ibid, p. 77

[30]Ibid, pp. 619-620

[31]Bailey, Alice A., *Initiation Human and So*lar, London: Lucis Publishing Company, 1972, p.20

[32]Ibid, p. 21

[33]Ibid, p. 21

[34]Ibid, p. 22

[35]Ibid, p. 22

[36]Ibid, p. 24

[37]Ibid, p. 24

[38]Ibid, p. 25

[39]Ibid, pp. 28-29

[40]Ibid, p. 30

[41]Ibid, pp. 33-34

[42]Ibid, pp. 34-35

[43]Ibid, p. 35

[44]Bailey, Alice A., *Education in the New Age,* London: Lucis Publishing Company, 1951, 117

[45]Bailey, Alice A., *Externalization of the Hierarchy*, London: Lucis Press Ltd., 1939, p.226

[46]Ibid, pp. 680-681

[47]Bailey, Alice A., *Education in the New Age*, London: Lucis Publishing Company, 1951, 118

[48]Ibid, p.118 [49]Ibid. p.119 [50]Ibid. p. 122

[51]Bailey, Alice A., *Externalization of the Hierarchy*, London: Lucis Press Ltd., 1939, pp. 594-595

[52]Ibid, pp. 688-689

[53]Ibid, p. 362

[54]Ibid, p. 268

Chapter Six

[1]Liebstoeckl, Hans, *In the Light of Our Time*, London: Rider and Company, 1931, p.7

[2]Besant, Annie, *The Building of the Kosmos*, London: Theosophical Publishing Company, 1894, p.29

[3]Ibid, p. 33

[4]Ibid, p. 53

[5]Ibid, p. 27

[6]Ibid, p. 41

[7]Case, Paul Foster, *The Tarot: A Key to the Wisdom of the Ages*, Los Angeles: Builders of the Adytum, 1990, p.169

[8]Besant, Annie, *The Building of the Kosmos*, London: Theosophical Publishing Company, 1894, p.52 [9]Case, Paul Foster, *The Tarot: A Key to the Wisdom of the Ages*, Los Angeles: Builders of the Adytum, 1990, p.39

[10]Ibid, p. 50

[11]Ibid, p. 58

[12]Fortune, Dion, *The Mystical Kabalah*, Maine: Samuel Wiser Inc., 1984, p.255

[13]Case, Paul Foster, *The Tarot: A Key to the Wisdom of the Ages*, Los Angeles: Builders of the Adytum, 1990, p 58

[14]Ibid, p. 192

[15]Ibid, p. 119

[16]Ibid, p.205

[17]Bailey, Alice A., *Esoteric Astrology*, London: Lucis Publishing Company, 1951, p. 481

[18]Levi, Eliphas, *The Book of Splendors*, Great Britain: The Aquarian Press and Samuel Wiser Inc., 1973, p.160

[19]Blavatsky, H. P., *Secret Doctrine, vol.II*, Pasedena: Theosophical University Press, 1970, p. 249

[20]Ibid, p. 250

[21]Hall, Manly P., *Masonic, Hermetic, Qabalistic and Rosicrucian Symbolical Philosophy*, Los Angeles: The Philosophical Research Society Press, 1936, p.XLIV

[22]Case, Paul Foster, *The Tarot: A Key to the Wisdom of the Ages*, Los Angeles: Builders of the Adytum, 1990, p.44

[23]Hall, Manly P., *Masonic, Hermetic, Qabalistic and Rosicrucian Symbolical Philosophy*, Los Angeles: The Philosophical Research Society Press, 1936, p. LXXVI

[24]Ibid, p. LXXVI

[25]Ibid, p. LXXIII

[26]Ibid, p. LXXIII

[27]Ibid, p. LXXIV

[28]Ibid, p. LXXIV

[29]Ibid, p. LXXV

Chapter Seven

[1]Bailey, Alice A., *The Consciousness of the Atom*, London: Lucis Publishing Company, 1952, p. 87

[2]Bailey, Alice A., *The Light of the Soul*, New York: Lucis Publishing Company, 1988, p.173

[3]Ibid, p. 74

[4]Ibid, p. 172

[5]Bailey, Alice A., *Initiation Human and Solar*, New York: Lucis Publishing Company, 1972, p. 20

[6]Case, Paul Foster, *The Tarot: A Key to the Wisdom of the Ages*, Los Angeles: Builders of the Adytum, 1990,p. 45

[7]Ibid, p. 103

[8]Ibid, p. 161

[9]Ibid, p. 49

[10]Three Initiates, *The Kybalion*, Chicago: The Yogi Publication Society, Masonic Temple, 1940, p. 25 [11]Case, Paul Foster, *The Tarot: A Key to the Wisdom of the Ages*, Los Angeles: Builders of the Adytum, 1990, p. 111

[12]Ibid, p. 169

[13]Ibid, p. 57

[14]Ibid, p. 119

[15]Ibid, p. 175

[16]Ibid, p. 65

[17]Ibid, p. 127

[18]Ibid, p. 183

[19]Ibid, p. 75

[20]Ibid, p. 135

[21]Ibid, p. 191

[22]Ibid, p. 85

[23]Ibid, p. 199

[24]Ibid, p. 93

[25]Ibid, p. 153

[26]Ibid, p. 205

[27]Three Initiates, *The Kybalion*, Chicago: The Yogi Publication Society, Masonic Temple, 1940, p. 115

Glossary of Terms

Adam Kadmon: the regenerated man that the fully lighted Tree of Life depicts

Adept: a human being who has traveled the path of evolution and has entered the final stage on the Path of Initiation. He has passed into the fifth kingdom and is now God-Man

Akasha: the third sphere of the supernal triangle out of which the idea for the manifestation of Spirit into matter emanated. It is called the mixing bowl for the colors and vibrations present in form

Alchemy: the process by which based metal is turned to silver and gold. The cauldron is the human body in which the process of transmutation takes place by fire in water, with the aid of the mind. The process is the evolution of consciousness

Alcyone: one of the seven Pleiades and is called the star of intelligence or the star of the individual. Its energies penetrate and impregnate the substance of the universe with the quality of mind

Androgyne: the One undifferentiated Intelligence before separation into its negative and positive polarities.

Angel of the Presence: Archangel Michael, the solar angel who stands face-to-face with the Dweller on the Threshold at the aspirant's initiation to distribute the solar fire

Aquarian Age: the next 2,500 year period in which humanity will bring about the spiritualization of matter and the occult teachings will be externalized and made more available to the masses

Aryan: a member of the fifth root race that includes the Hindu peoples, the peoples of Europe and modern America

Ascended Master: one who has traveled the road of illumination and achieved Illumination; s/he is now a member of the Hierarchy who serves in the liberation of humanity

Astrology: the science of the relationships that exist between all living organisms within the universe.

Atlantis: the continent that followed the Lemurian civilization; it was located, according to Plato, in the Atlantic Ocean and was home of the fourth root race called the Atlanteans.

Cardinal: beginning or initiating in quality as in the four cardinal signs: Aries, Cancer, Libra and Capricorn, which also denotes the beginning of the four seasons

Chakras: seven vortices or wheels of energy that work in association with the endocrine glands on man's physical, emotional and mental bodies toward his development.

Christ Consciousness: that stage in man's evolution where duality ends

Chyle: the milky, fatty, liquid substance produced in the small intestines during the process of assimilation in the Virgo region of the body; called liquid gold, this substance travels through the blood stream and is essential in the spiritual unfoldment of the aspirant

Consciousness: the responses and reactions of the individual to the forces of the twelve constellations and the twelve planets impacting him. This leads to the development of the life of the soul toward the will-to-power, the will-to-love and the will-to-know

Cosmic: relating to a consciousness that is beyond the planetary scheme; the individuals who have attained this level of consciousness work on both the planetary and universal levels of the divine plan

Decantes: the three sub-divisions under each of the 12 signs of the zodiac; there are, therefore, thirty-six decants.

Devil: the veiled aspect of Archangel Michael; the mental creation of mankind; the repository of mankind's fears and ignorance.

Emanations: the ten outward expressions of the "One about which naught can be said." These are called Sephiroth on the Tree of Life.

Endocrine glands: seven ductless glands generally aligned with the spine and are associated with the seven vortices of energy called chakras. They play a vital role in the evolution of man.

Enlightenment: see Illumination

Esoteric: that which pertains to the knowledge and study of the energies and forces which affect the consciousness aspect of the human being and is concerned with the soul.

Exoteric: knowledge and study of the personality.

Eve: symbol of the mental aspect and the mind of man; attracted by the lure of knowledge to be gained through the experience of incarnation.

Evolution: the inter-relation between God and his creation, cause and effect, spirit and matter, and the transformation that results from divine attraction. The aim of the process is to shield, nurture and reveal the hidden spiritual reality, which veils form.

Fifth Principle: the principle of mind; that faculty in man, which is the intelligent thinking principle that differentiates man from the animals.

Freemasonry: that brotherhood to which every member of the human family belongs; the largest organization in the world and prepares candidates for the inward life.

God-Man: the liberated man in whom the personality and the soul are fused and is conditioned by the divine plan and its purpose.

Great Bear, the: the constellation influencing the first emanation of the Divine Triad, which contained the divine idea of the plan to be carried out in matter. The seven brothers issue from this sphere.

Great Work, the: the process by which the merge of the personality and the soul takes place; the occultists say that this is accomplished by the Sun and the Moon with the aid of Mercury, or thoughts and feelings with the aid of the mind.

Hermes Trismegistus: the Thrice Great was the messenger of the gods to man and is said to have brought writing, medicine and civilization to Earth; He embodies in himself both aspects of the mental principle, the expression of the concrete, and the abstract mind of God.

Hexagram: this six-pointed geometric symbol of two triangles fused, one ascending and the other descending and is called the Star of David; interlaced, it is called Solomon's seal; it represents the merging of the Soul and the Personality in the completion of the Great Work.

Hierarchy, the: a group of spiritual beings on the inner planes of the solar system who control the evolutionary process. They are divided into twelve hierarchies. A reflection of this Hierarchy is called the occult hierarchy and is made up of adepts and initiates.

Hiram Abiff: the symbol of Masonry representing the Master-Builder and Grandmaster entrusted with the building of Solomon's Temple; He is the symbolic embodiment of the Lost Word; he has the Light and is, therefore, the Triune Self and the four elements combined; his life, death, and resurrection illustrates the story of Masonry and the destiny of humanity; He is the Master Mason who is symbolic of Hermes and Jesus.

Illumination: the synthesis of instinct, intellect and intuition in the Pilgrim brought about by mental unfoldment, which produces in him the final stage of mental evolution along the Path of Initiation.

Initiate: he is the man/woman in whom there is an absence of dualism. He can stand at the center of the transforming will and bring about the needed changes in the form nature without identifying himself with it or being affected by it. His number is eleven and he works in the eleventh sign of the zodiac, Aquarius, the sign of universal consciousness.

Initiation: the process of penetrating into the mysteries of the science of the Self and of one's self in all senses. The Path of Initiation is the final stage in the evolution traveled by man and is divided into seven stages represented by the seven gateways of the charkas.

Intuition: the ability to arrive at knowledge through the link established between the personality and the soul. It is achieved through the extension of the reasoning faculty; it is the sense of synthesis; the ability to think in wholes and to touch the world of causes.

Involution: the path taken by spirit through the four worlds to be solidly immersed into matter.

Isis: one of the three aspects of the Virgin Mother; She symbolizes the aspect of the form nature called the personality vehicle and specifically the manifestation of the Christ child on the emotional or astral plane.

Israel: the peoples of the Earth who are descendants of the three older brothers of the Race; they are: Arabs, Semites, Afghans, Moors, Latin and Celtic peoples; Teutons, Scandinavians and Anglo-Saxons.

Jerusalem: that place symbolically in the individual, country, the world where death to separation and ignorance takes place; it is also a city of peace; that place arrived at by the regenerated consciousness; the sign of Pisces, is therefore, symbolically Jerusalem.

Jews: being of the tribe of Judah bearing certain spiritual characteristics and having divine responsibilities; they are a remnant of the all the peoples and races of the world.

Kumaras: the highest seven self-conscious beings in the solar system; they are the sum-total of intelligence and of wisdom. They manifest on Earth through seven planetary schemes as humans manifest in physical bodies.

Kundalini: the coiled-up serpent energy at the base of the spine that eventually unfurls during the process of spiritual awakening. This force opens the spiritual centers along the spine, releasing spiritual fire, which activates the centers in the head for receiving the higher knowledge into the body.

Kuthumi: Master of the second ray of Love and Wisdom and the emerging World Teacher in charge of education and religion.

Lemuria: the continent, which preceded Atlantis and was the home of the third root race.

Lodge, the: as a room it is an oblong square and represents one-half of a perfect square and the lower half of a circle. These are symbolic of the un-regenerated man who is not yet "whole". Similarly, the planet Earth and the human body are considered a "Lodge" and are moving toward wholeness. When the candidate becomes a Master Mason, he has "squared the circle" and has become the perfect stone and the "chief corner stone", a cube. He is now the "Keystone".

Logos: the Deity who manifests through every nation and people. Metaphysically, speech is the logos of thought and is translated as the "word".

Lucifer: the Sun of the morning and the head of the Center of Humanity; the prince of the power of the Air; the twin aspect of Archangel Michael.

Mary: the third of the three goddesses related to the mother aspect, which brought the Christ child down to the plane of incarnation, the physical plane.

Master Mason: the man or woman who has taken the final initiation and has become an adept of whom Hiram Abiff is a type. S/he is the Knower and Master Builder of the Lodge.

Maya: (illusion.) Any phenomenon or objective appearance created by the mind

Melchizedek: the Ancient of Days or the Great High Priest.

Mercury: the Roman name for Thoth or Hermes. (see Hermes and Thoth)

Monad: the "One" or threefold aspect of the supernal Triune; the Spirit or immortal part of man.

Moon Center, the: associated with the sixth chakra and the pituitary gland. This center oversees the development of all forms.

Mutable: changeable, transitional; the quality of mediation as with the four mutable signs of the zodiac: Pisces, Gemini, Virgo, and Sagittarius.

New World Order: the hierarchy of the Masters of Wisdom who are externalizing and will sit in positions of power in all our systems of government. They will oversee the liberation of humanity.

Oversoul: the collective guiding entity of all humanity also called the Higher Self, which oversees and directs the evolution of all life on Earth

Path of Return: the conscious path of humanity in the journey back into full consciousness along the thirty-two paths of wisdom

Pentagram: the five-pointed geometric symbol of spirit and its dominion over matter: fire, water, air and earth

Personality vehicle: the combined physical, emotional and mental bodies

Pleiades: the constellation representing the third aspect of the Godhead. It is associated with Binah on the Tree of Life. The Pleiades is also called the seven sisters or the seven rays of life energy manifesting on our planet.

Planets: the 12 known bodies of energy forces in the solar system that impact the growth and evolution of all life on Earth. There are seven sacred and five non-sacred planets, which include Vulcan and Earth.

Prima Materia: alchemical water, the primal substance from which all life emerged.

Principles, Seven Hermetic: the seven divine laws on which manifestation is established. They are mentalism, correspondence, vibration, polarity, rhythm, cause and effect and gender.

Prodigal Son: a symbol for humanity and the wandering Jew who left his father's house to achieve an expansion of consciousness through experiment and experience.

Qabalah: this traditional Hermetic and Judaic science has been called the mathematics of human thought. It is the algebra of faith that solves all problems of the soul as equations by isolating the unknowns.

It brings to ideas the clarity and rigorous exactitude of numbers. Its results for the mind are infallibility, relative to the sphere of human knowledge, and for the heart it provides profound peace.

Quintessence: Spirit, the essence of all there is.

Raphael, archangel: the archangel who rules the eastern quadrant of the heavens. "God, the Healer-of- Mind."

Rays: the seven streams of force or great lights of the Logos. Each of them is the embodiment of a great cosmic entity.

Razor's Edge, the: the balancing middle path the aspirant must walk toward enlightenment.

Root race: one of the seven races of man that evolve upon a planet during the cycle of planetary existence. Each cycle is called a world period. We are now in the 5th world cycle of the Aryan root race that includes the Hindu, European and peoples of modern America.

Saint Germaine: also known as Master Rakozci; Master of the 7th Ray, Alchemy and Ceremonial Order. He is overseer of the Aquarian Age, sponsor of the United States, Europe and Australia; Master of civilization and is the Chief Master Mason; architect of the business and financial world in Europe and America.

Sanat Kumara: the head of the seven Kumaras who came into the Earth plane. He corresponds to the Great Bear from which the initiating principle is projected. In the Qabalistic system this Being is called Metatron.

Scarab: the esoteric replacement for the crab. It is also the symbol for the aspirant as he evolves on the upward spiral of the Wheel of Life.

Self-consciousness: the awareness in the individual of purpose, of a self-directed life, a developed and definite life-plan and program. These are indicative of some measure of integration and mental perception.

Shamballah: the city of the Gods and home of the mystical occult doctrine; the custodian of the plan for our planet.

Sirius: called the "dog star". Vibrations from Sirius reach our planet via the cosmic mental plane. It is the Star of Sensitivity governing the Hierarchy.

Solomon's Seal: the interlaced Star of David or hexagram.

Solomon's Temple: a symbolic form of the deathless physical body not made with hands and built out of the ruins of the previously destroyed temples, the personality and the soul; Finally the Master Mason or Hiram Abiff stands as that perfected Temple

Soul, the: the Higher Self or Higher Mind. It projects out into form through the personality vehicle to be used for carrying out of the divine plan in matter. It is the medium between Spirit and Matter.

Ultimately, it too must die.

Swastika: the mutable cross of material change and constant movement. The swastika can be a symbol for evil and the false use of matter.

Tarot, Qabalistic: seventy-eight cards containing the knowledge of the whole universe; Man and the universe in pictorial symbols.

Thoth: the Egyptian name given to Hermes Trismegistus, the Thrice Great. (see also Hermes and Mercury).

Tree of Life: the glyph of man and the universe. This geometric symbol consists of ten Sephiroth or emanations and twenty-two secret paths, constituting the thirty-two paths of wisdom.

Uranus: the ruler of the Age of Aquarius; producer of occult consciousness, which is the intelligent fusing condition, which produces the scientific at-one-ment of the higher and lower selves through the intelligent use of the mind.

Venus: the alter ego of the planet Earth; the mental energy of humanity that establishes relation from man- to-man and nation-to-nation. Venus is to Earth what the Higher Self is to the Personality.

Via Delorosa: the path of sorrow every aspirant travels toward the liberation of Spirit out of the bondage of matter.

Vulcan: the esoteric ruler of Taurus. It is one of the seven sacred planets and rules the inner man and guides his development at the first initiation or early stages of his spiritual unfoldment.

Selected Bibliography

Armstrong, Herbert W., *The United States and Britain in Prophecy*, Pasadena: Worldwide Church of God, 1980.

Bailey, Alice A., *The Consciousness of the Atom*, New York: Lucis Publishing Company, 1922

_____, *Destiny of the Nations*, London: Lucis Publishing Company, 1952

_____, *Education in the New Age*, London: Lucis Publishing Company, 1951

_____, *Esoteric Astrology*, New York: Lucis Publishing Company, 1951

_____, *Esoteric Psychology*, London: Lucis Publishing Company, 1952

_____, *Externalization of the Hierarchy*, New York: Lucis Publishing Company, 1957.

_____, *Initiation Human and Solar*, London: Lucis Publishing Company, 1957

_____, *The Labors of Hercules*, An Astrological Interpretation, London: 1974

_____, *Light of the Soul*, New York: Lucis Publishing Company, 1988

Besant, Annie, *The Building of the Kosmos*, London: The Theosophical Publishing Society, 1894 Blavatsky, H. P, *The Secret Doctrine*, vol. II, Pasadena: The Theosophical University Press, 1970 Case, Paul Foster, *The Book of Tokens*, Los Angeles: Builders of the Adytum, 1989

Case, Paul Foster, *The Tarot: Key to the Wisdom of the Ancients*, Los Angeles: Builders of the Adytum, 1990 Fortune, Dion, *The Mystical Qabalah*, Maine: Samuel Wiser, Inc., 1984

Hall, Manly P., *The Lost Key of Masonry*, Los Angeles: The Philosophical Research Society, 1932

Hall, Manly P., *Masonic, Hermetic, Qabalah and Rosicrucian Symbolic Philosophy*, Los Angeles: The Philosophical Research Society Press, 1936

Levi, Eliphas, *The Book of Splendors*, Great Britain: The Aquarian Press and Samuel Wiser Inc., 1973 Three Initiates, *The Kybalion*, Chicago: The Yogi Publication Society, Masonic Temple, 1940 Wilmshurst, W. L. *The Meaning of Masonry*, London: Watkins Publishers, 1932

Recommendations for Spiritual Training

1. Builders of the Adytum: 5101-5 N.
    Figueroa Street Los Angeles, CA 90042 U.S.A.
    Phone: 1 (323) 255- 7141
    Fax: 1 (323) 255-4166

2. Builders of the Adytum: New Zealand
    also serving Australia and the South Pacific.
    Contact: (04) 567 5751,
    or email bota@xtra.co.nz.

3. Builders of the Adytum:
    Europe B.O.T.A. 16 Boulevard Saint Assiscle
    66000 Perpignan FRANCE;
    Tel.: (33) 4 68 87 21 09
    E-Mail: europe@bota.org

    And

4. The Arcane School, The Lucis Trust:
    866 United Nations Plaza, FL New York, NY 10017 U.S.A.
    Contact: Phone: + 1 (212) 292 0707
    Fax: +1 (212) 292 0808
    Contact: Tel: +1 (212) 292-0707;
    Fax: +1 (212) 292-0808;
    E-mail: newyork@lucistrust.org

5. 3 Whitehall Court, Suite 54, London SW1A 2EF UK
    Contact: Tel: +44 (0)20 7839 4512;
    Fax: +44 (0)20 7839 5575;
    E-mail: london@lucistrust.org

6. The Arcane School, The Lucis Trust: Rue du Stand 40,
    Case Postale 5323
    1211 Geneva 11, Switzerland;
    Contact: Tel: +41 (22) 734-1252;
    E-mail: geneva@lucistrust.org

Index

About the Author

Photo by Don Parchment

Understanding Your Choice was written to answer some of the great perplexing questions of our time. Have you ever contemplated the great mysteries of life and asked: What is life about? Who am I? What is my destiny? Where am I going? Etta D. Jackson has first-hand knowledge and experience about these subjects she writes about in 'Understanding Your Choice'. She has had a deep knowing of the inner meaning of life on many planes and dimensions of existence since her early childhood. She has always known on the deepest levels of her being, the Oneness of all life, and that all differences are only parts of the One Unifying Whole. She shares with you in this book the fact that Man is, in fact, the great mystery that he has been searching for; and that in knowing himself he comes to know God. It is her firm belief that Man's primary purpose on Earth is to answer these deep questions and in doing so he will come to know himself. In this knowing, separation of all kind ends, and he comes to know his true relationship to God and his fellowman.

Etta holds a B.A. degree in Biology; M.S. degrees in Psychoanalytic Counseling and Development as well as in Administrative Leadership and Supervision and is currently a Ph.D. student in Leadership and Change. Through her work as school district coordinator for the desegregation program in a suburban school district, she had the opportunity to gain added insights into the many issues that divide and separate peoples; she came to the clear understanding of the deep separateness held in the collective psyche of humanity.

In 1986 she became a student of an Ancient Mystery School, which has been invaluable in providing her with a deeper intellectual understanding of the great mysteries and added to the innate knowing she had as a child. She has a daughter and a grandson.

Printed in Great Britain
by Amazon

56034465R00167